Everybody's Got a
Seed to Sow

The Brookwood Story

"Everybody's Got A Seed to Sow, is the amazing story of one family's journey to provide a life of meaning for their brain damaged sister and daughter, Vicki. Finding no resources to meet those needs, they set out to create them. Overcoming insurmountable obstacles with the help of friends and a strong faith, these efforts have changed the face of education. A pathway was created for Vicki, and others, to learn and grow...as we deal with the curveballs of life!"

> **– SUSAN G. BAKER**
> **Author of *Passing It On***

"My wife and I did not know what to expect when we visited Brookwood but we were inspired by the vision that has shaped this amazing God-given place. We have travelled the world extensively and can say with confidence that there is nothing like it anywhere. It deserves our total support."

> **– LORD AND LADY CAREY**
> **103rd Archbishop of Canterbury**

"In a perfect world, everyone is valuable...viable...virtuous and victorious. We know that there is no such thing as a perfect world but something close to it exists at The Brookwood Community. "So often we focus on the end game and forget the journey it took to get there. The story of Brookwood reminds us of what can happen, when you truly believe it can. Our struggle is our strength and faith is the foundation upon which it rests."

> **– DEBORAH DUNCAN**
> **Senior Producer/Host, "Great Day Houston", KHOU-TV CBS**

"Everybody's Got a Seed to Sow is a good thought during the week and a spiritual thought on Sunday's; but it is also the beautiful story of how a true treasure, The Brookwood Community, came to be. This story of love and inspiration will renew your faith in humanity as it answers the question, what does *special* mean if everyone is *special*? Brookwood, sowing one seed after another, provides us with that answer."

– **MIKE FEINBERG**
  Co-Founder, KIPP

"The citizens of Brookwood have been a real inspiration to me. They demonstrate that people with special needs can live a life filled with purpose, contribute to society and enjoy a real sense of community. Brookwood is a nonprofit that is run like a business. Every time I visit Brookwood I leave feeling inspired by what I've seen. It is a model that is worth emulating."

– **SCOTT McCLELLAND**
  President, H-E-B Houston

"Everybody's Got a Seed to Sow, The Brookwood Story is a riveting book about caring for people with special needs. Brookwood believes, as I do, that work is not a right it is a human instinct. Please read *Everybody's Got a Seed to Sow* as it will inspire and challenge you as Brookwood has inspired me."

– **JIM McINGVALE**
  Entrepreneur

"This book will inspire, inform, and change you. There are many wonderful ideas on how to make life better for those with disabilities and not only are the ideas creative but the approaches are remarkably comprehensive. You will see how making a good life is not about just having programs but also about having meaningful work and helping each individual to view themselves as competent and worthwhile and someone who can contribute to their community when given the opportunity and treated with respect."

> – **GARY B. MESIBOV**
> **Ph.D. Professor Emeritus, University of North Carolina at Chapel Hill**

"I toured the Brookwood Community, talked to the citizens, admired their work and saw the commitment the staff had to ensuring all citizens had a sense of community and belonging, and that their lives were about living with dignity and respect. The place has such a magical feel and reputation that the surrounding Houston area frequently comes to visit the Brookwood Community; they eat in the restaurant, shop in the gift store or greenhouses and some become volunteers. The citizens are active; work every day at their real and important jobs, some reside at Brookwood, and other citizens come to the campus to work just for the day. "

> – **CYNTHIA PEACOCK, MD, FAAP, FACP**
> **Medical Director, Baylor College of Medicine – Texas Children's Hospital Transition Medicine Clinic**
> **Director, Center for Transition Medicine in the Department of Medicine at Baylor College of Medicine**

"I have never experienced anything quite like Brookwood. I have visited many communities that minister to adults with functional disabilities, but Brookwood is the only one where Brookwood "citizens" live, work, and play in an environment that creates significant dignity, worth, and respect.

The work of the citizens is not token work. It is meaningful work that produces excellent products that people want to purchase. The work creates dignity and worth; and, the products help sustain the citizen's community. That pride in their unique abilities helps them grow socially, emotionally, and spiritually."

> – **DR. JOHN E. STEPHENS**
> **Senior Pastor, Chapelwood United Methodist Church**

"This is a wonderful story of a family's unconditional love for their daughter, but more than that, it's the story of the creation of a Houston institution. What an inspiration."

> – **STEVE STEVENS**
> **Past Chairman, Houston Livestock Show & Rodeo**

"I am delighted to commend *Everybody's Got a Seed to Sow*. At Brookwood, the spirit soars, and this book is written in that same spirit of soaring. This story, which includes family, friends, and wise guides, is delightful and inspirational. It is a real-life encounter of faith, hard-won wisdom, perseverance, and generous love. The Brookwood story needs to be told and yearns to be heard."

> – **JERRY WEBBER**
> **The Center for Christian Spirituality, Chapelwood United Methodist Church**

bright sky press
HOUSTON, TEXAS

2365 Rice Blvd., Suite 202
Houston, Texas 77005

10 9   8   7   6   5   4   3   2   1

Library of Congress Cataloging-in-Publication Data on file with publisher.

ISBN 978-1-939055-78-1

Editorial Direction: Lucy Herring Chambers
Managing Editor: Lauren Gow
Designer: Marla Y. Garcia
Cover Illustration: Bubuka Designs by Yara Suki
Back Cover Photo: Rossitsa Israel, 1.618 Multimedia

Printed in Canada through Friesens

Everybody's Got a
Seed to Sow

The Brookwood Story

YVONNE T. STREIT
with JANA MULLINS

bright sky press

HOUSTON, TEXAS

Through the grace of God,
the Brookwood Community provides
opportunities for growth educationally,
emotionally, vocationally, and spiritually
for adults with special needs.

We offer our grateful appreciation to our underwriters
whose gifts for the publishing of this book allow
the proceeds from the sale of each copy to go to Brookwood,
its citizens, and its outreach programs.

Nancy and Bud Simpson

──────────

Michael and Janet Montgomery
The Light Charitable Trust

Some people walk
Some people race
Some people vary in their pace
However there is One thing I know
Everybody's got a seed to sow

– **M I C H A E L   W .   S M I T H**

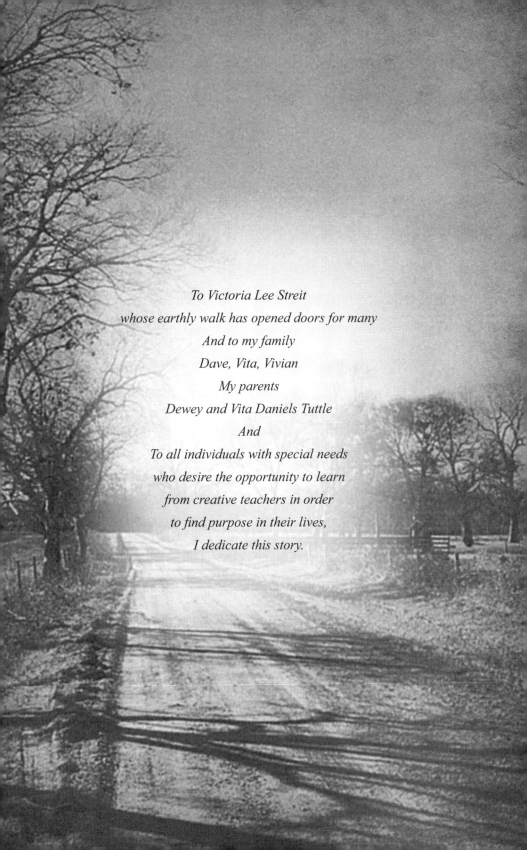

To Victoria Lee Streit
whose earthly walk has opened doors for many
And to my family
Dave, Vita, Vivian
My parents
Dewey and Vita Daniels Tuttle
And
To all individuals with special needs
who desire the opportunity to learn
from creative teachers in order
to find purpose in their lives,
I dedicate this story.

TABLE OF CONTENTS

FOREWORD *14*

INTRODUCTION *18*

I. SEEDS *23*

II. SPROUTS *53*

III. ROOTS *101*

IV. BLOSSOMS *179*

APPENDIX *211*

ACKNOWLEDGEMENTS *222*

God's chair in the Worship Center.

FOREWORD

I first came to The Brookwood Community in 1985, invited by Yvonne Streit to speak at the dedication of this dream come true. I had been encouraged by a good friend whose disabled daughter had found a happy home there after a sometimes-painful search. Since then, I have been heartened to see the work of this dedicated group flourish. Although the impressive campus today looks very little like the small community I visited initially, the values, the work ethic, and the spirit remain the same.

Where many would look at a group of functionally disabled adults and see people who deserve society's pity, Brookwood has overcome that stereotype and created a community that epitomizes the Texas can-do spirit. The citizens understand that their efforts matter, that they are valuable, and that they are not just being kept safe or out of sight. They earn paychecks, grow and sell beautiful plants, and create useful and highly marketable products. While they are not able to accomplish these things in the regular way, they learn that they each have gifts that can be used in tandem with the gifts of others to surpass perceived limitations. Together, with this wonderful sense of interdependence, they create many useful items and generate a significant portion of Brookwood's expenses—but the most important thing they create is the sense of possibility and purpose.

What good is a functionally disabled adult to society? Brookwood shows us that the possibilities are endless. It is heartening to see how this community has grown from the early days and how it continues to develop—spreading its understanding of the relationship of work to self-esteem, its acceptance of each individual as he or she is created, and its indomitable love of life in all its surprising manifestations.

Ralph Waldo Emerson once asked, "What is a weed?" He answered the question in a way particularly appropriate to this place so renowned for its horticulture. A weed, he determined, is "a plant whose virtues have not yet been discovered." The Brookwood Community has recognized the virtues of a group of people who were generally disdained by society until the middle of the twentieth century and built a community for them that serves as an example to us all. The insights that Yvonne has gained on this journey are important for this group of individuals and can teach all of us more compassionate and productive ways to treat each other and ourselves.

As the story that follows will show you, it was not an easy journey. A mother's love knows no limits, and the work that was put in motion when Yvonne determined to help her youngest daughter formed a team, which in turn formed a strong foundation for this place. People here are valued for who they are and what they can contribute, not judged for their perceived shortcomings. Wouldn't it be wonderful if everyone received this kind of respect? What potential could be unlocked, and what problems could be solved? The Brookwood story reminds us how important meaningful work is and underlines the value of each person's contribution to the community. We all have a seed to sow, a light to shine, a gift to offer—and with the magic of interdependence and creative teachers, that seed can be found and planted. We need to provide each other with the opportunities to strengthen our communities through contributions such as these.

Barbara Bush

HOUSTON, TEXAS 2016

Staff and citizen homes.

INTRODUCTION

T his is a story about God, our family, and a continuing miracle called The Brookwood Community. Brookwood is a God-centered, educational community for adults with special needs—a place designed to enhance the lives of these individuals, to provide them purpose, meaningful work and a fulfilling life. Without our youngest daughter Vicki, Brookwood might not be here. As Vicki's mother, I have walked this journey with her and have been blessed to see the hand and heart of God in each and every step we have taken. We didn't have a place like Brookwood in mind at the beginning—not even as a dream. To my knowledge, such places didn't exist. But as we sought to help Vicki and others like her, we found ourselves on the road to what would one day become an answer to prayer.

For years people have encouraged me to tell the story of The Brookwood Community from my perspective, and for years I have resisted. It's not that I'm stubborn (ha-ha!) or that I wouldn't know how to write a book. It's more an awareness that it's not just *my* story to tell. You see, Brookwood's story belongs to every single person who has crossed its threshold, and even to some who have not. I once heard that if you are on the inside of an astounding experience, you don't know how to explain it; and if you are on the outside, you can't always understand it. Something that is *indescribable yet undeniable.* That's how the Brookwood story has felt to me. It's like a jigsaw puzzle, where all the pieces, large and small, are important. It is a complex, emotional, wonderful story, overwhelmingly powered by God's presence and by the gifts of others.

The past five decades have been such a wild rollercoaster ride that I've seldom taken the time to think back on all that has happened, much less put it in perspective. Every so often I have been persuaded to sit down with a tape recorder and recall some of the miraculous, moving stories that have formed this community. What finally convinced me to put my version of Brookwood's history on the printed page was that I realized no one else still here has lived it from the beginning as my family has. If I don't share it now, the stories of God's activity here, the wonderful lessons we have learned along the way, and the contributions of individual Brookwoodians might be forgotten. That would be a shame. My husband, Dave, our daughters Vita and Vivian, and our daughter, Vicki—if she could talk—would no doubt tell slightly different versions of this story. And they would probably be equally true.

These are the facts about Brookwood as I have experienced them. I am painfully aware that for every story I tell of the loving generosity and strength of others, there are dozens more I may have forgotten. I am beyond grateful for the individuals and institutions who have given thousands of hours and millions of dollars to help Brookwood grow and flourish. I am also grateful for those who might have given a lawnmower or even pushed it (yes, our first lawn mower was the old push type), or played with Vicki so I could work with another child, or invited a future donor or citizen's family to come out for a tour. Each and every contribution has its own special place in the formation of this community. I am perpetually humbled by the love and understanding that inspired and continues to inspire those gifts.

My journey to Brookwood began in 1957, when our one-year-old daughter became seriously disabled. But who's to say that our family wasn't already on this path and Vicki's desperate situation just woke us up to it? Like the proverbial turtle on the fencepost, I don't really need to know *why* I got here; I just need to acknowledge the One who put me here. There has clearly been a divine purpose at work—even though that purpose wasn't clear to me in the beginning.

When people introduce me to make speeches and such, they often call me the woman who founded Brookwood. I just laugh and tell them the truth: *God is the founder of Brookwood. I just work for Him.* I didn't apply for the job, and it came without a business plan or a policies-and-procedures manual. I have been training on-the-job from the very first day, and over a period of time this work has taught me clearly that we each have a purpose: *everybody's got a seed to sow.* What follows here is a Brookwood story, but it's not the whole story. The story of this community is ever-evolving, and there are as many Brookwood stories as there are Brookwoodians and friends of Brookwood—each one with a unique point of view…and…each one with a special seed to sow.

Yvonne Streit

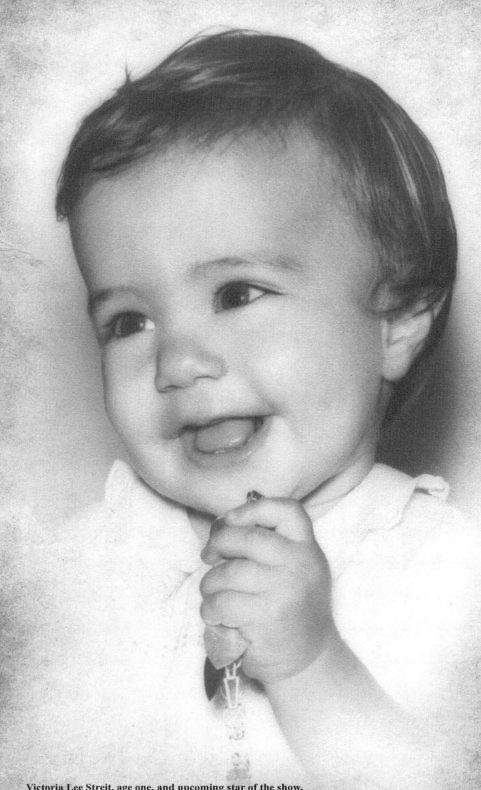

**Victoria Lee Streit, age one, and upcoming star of the show,
just weeks before the onset of her illness.**

I.

S E E D S

Each one of us is shaped by our environment. The home into which we're born, our parents, *their* parents, the development of habits and individual character traits: all of these may determine our future. Some of these influences are good; others are not so good. Human beings such as I, may demonstrate selfishness, weakness, ego, avoidance, denial, lack of discipline, and ignorance, *as well as* generosity, determination, perseverance, hopefulness, helpfulness, visionary gifts, and good old common sense. In other words, we're a pretty mixed bag!

I can see now that my own life has been shaped by many of the lessons I learned as a child. Some were intentionally taught; others were caught. Those lessons quite naturally came from my parents (good parenting is so important), as well as from others—teachers, extended family, friends, and neighbors. As I look back on the path that led our family to Brookwood, I see that God's hand has been in each and every facet of this journey—when I was aware of His presence, and when I was not. He provided both the seeds and the fertile soil where they might grow. He protected and pruned and watered, but I was mostly unaware at first. But as time went on, there were more and more days when I would simply shake my head in amazement and think, "Thank you Father. I know you're in the midst of this."

FAMILY TREE

I grew up with two loving parents and a brother on a shady street in a nice Houston neighborhood. Our family was extraordinary in some ways yet very ordinary in others. As a little girl, the grown-up life I envisioned for myself centered on hearth and home, playing a little tennis and bridge, volunteering in the community, and helping out at whatever school my healthy, happy children might attend. In my mind that's where I was headed, because that was what I saw around me. Looking back, it amazes me how many different, everyday situations my parents used as opportunities to guide my brother Lee and me. Not that we learned from all of these, but many lessons *did* stick with us and turned out to be very important for the path ahead.

Mother and Dad modeled to us what had been modeled to them. My mother's dad, Edward Sidney Daniels, was a ship's captain in the early 1900s. He had owned several trading ships that were lost in the storms of 1894, 1898, and 1900 before he began serving as a pilot on a tugboat that guided bigger vessels into and out of the port of Galveston. His work required discipline, precision, and careful attention to procedure—values he embodied at home. My mother's mother, Myra Holt Daniels, was probably one of the premier volunteers and Methodist church "starter-uppers" in the Upper Gulf Coast region. She brought innovative thinking, boundless energy, creativity, and determination to all that she did. Both my maternal grandparents had a deeply-embedded sense of doing for others, and this was epitomized by their actions. They walked the talk, and they remain in my heart as two of my heroes. I am so grateful that I had the opportunity to know them.

A product of her parents, my mother was a teacher—and, like her mother, a dedicated volunteer in many worthwhile causes. She served as president of several large volunteer organizations and met many challenges along the way—quite successfully, I might add.

On my father's side, my grandfather, William Edwin Tuttle, was a successful farmer but (and I was told) received a God nudge and became an itinerant Methodist minister in South Texas. The family of ten children was certainly not wealthy—so, out of necessity, all ten learned to work—and not just to work hard, but also work smart. Each one of those children demonstrated outstanding character and purpose.

My father desired at a very early age to get an education—and in those days public or free education was only available in the first few grades. High school education required money, and very few had the determination to pursue this goal. In spite of untold obstacles, my father began to work with determination toward that goal. He didn't wait for something to happen—he *made* it happen. He would drive a cart into San Antonio to sell strawberries (or whatever else he could find) in order to buy textbooks and pay for his lessons, which ultimately led him to become a doctor.

Both Mother and Dad wanted Lee, my brother, and me to realize what we had been given through the work of others and understand that it should never be taken for granted. Our first encounters with initiative and interdependence happened at home—and some of the most memorable of those teachable moments were very purposefully pointed out to us.

LESSONS FROM CHILDHOOD

From an early age, our parents provided for Lee's and my daily needs, but they wanted us to understand that they did not do so alone. There was the farmer who worked hard to plant and grow the food we bought; the automaker who designed and built the car; the carpenter who constructed the house; the garbage man who kept our neighborhood sanitary and free of trash, and so on. It was critical to our parents that we

> "Work is critically important to everyone, and it is not just an ethic, it is an instinct in all of us."

saw the ways in which each of us truly relies on others and how valuable everyone's work is. Noted psychologist Dr. James Hillman said, "Work is critically important to everyone, and it is not just an ethic, it is an instinct in all of us." My Mother and Dad certainly would have agreed!

While Lee and I were still children, my dad bought a piece of land between Houston and Galveston and tried his hand at farming. When he could get away from his "doctoring," he raised pigs and chickens. (At one point he had fifteen hundred chickens, and that was a mess!) Those chickens provided a major learning experience for all of us. They were a constant reminder to crawl before you try to walk, and walk before you try to run. The farm provided us with many other practical lessons as well.

In order to do the farming, we had a tractor; and by the time we were ten or eleven, we were taught how to drive it. Lee and I thought we were really something, driving that tractor and mowing the fields. Dad was quick to tell us that when he was a boy, his family didn't *have* a tractor. Eventually he had the *great* idea that Lee and I needed to experience what farm work was like before people (through determination and perseverance) developed this modern "tractor machine."

Dad introduced us to an old iron, hand-guided plow—the kind driven by a team of mules. But that presented a problem: we just had one mule. That did not deter my dad because we had a beautiful Tennessee Walker named Star Walker who was *my* horse. When Dad suggested we team Star Walker with the mule to pull the plow, I nearly had a fit. (I say "nearly" because fits of temper were not allowed in our house.) But as Dad so often insisted, we had to *adapt—learn to adjust*. When I continued to balk at his suggestion to turn my horse into half of a mule team, he posed the problem another way.

Learn to adapt—learn to adjust.

"Look at it like this," he said. "What would you do if you hadn't planned ahead, and you found out the hard way that you weren't going to have food if you didn't grow it, and to grow it you needed to use another animal? Would you still think that your horse was 'too good to pull a plow?'"

As quick as that, Star Walker became a member of the team—and quite a team it was! The mule responded to the reins one way and the Tennessee Walker another. After much futile effort at giving them equal play with the reins, I followed my mother's advice to "Try another way." Through trial and error I found that by wrapping the reins around my shoulders and hooking my elbows into them, I could give a stronger pull to the mule and a gentler one to the Tennessee Walker.

Mother was right. Whenever some well-intentioned effort would fail—whether social, emotional, academic, or vocational—there was almost always another way. And so it was with the plowing project. Plowing the old-fashioned way taught us another lesson, too. You know how you see those wonderful, straight, plowed rows when you're driving through the countryside? Well, our first efforts yielded not a single straight row: we had mostly curved ones, and more than a few that crisscrossed each other. The hard clay, not unusual in this part of the country, often turned us in a direction we did not mean to go. Needless to say, our crooked rows did not meet the minimum standard for quality that was required. So, not only did we have to "try another way," we had to try that other way over and over again, until we got it right.

"Do it right or don't do it," Dad would say. That did not mean perfection, but it did mean an effort toward excellence. I ought to clarify here that our parents did not view us as cheap labor. They merely asked us to do small portions of what needed to be done in order to experience as many facets of life as we could. Our folks saw to it that we had many opportunities to do just that—and generally we truly enjoyed them. So many of these *"little"* experiences became building blocks for my future life, which includes Briarwood and Brookwood.

Another one of those experiential learning opportunities came when my folks bought a boat. We would get in the boat and ride down to Galveston Bay and back—and that was exciting, but it was not as exciting as it might have been if we had an aquaplane to tow us behind the boat. For those of you too young to remember, an aquaplane was the "grandfather" of the wake board: a little platform, probably three-and-a-half to four feet long, about two-and-a-half feet wide, with a rope that you could hold on to, and another rope that went through a hole in the front of the aquaplane and attached to the boat.

When I insisted we needed one, my dad said, "Fine. Make one. If you want one, make it."

That had never entered my mind, but at Dad's challenge, I got started. I took two planks and actually cut them off (with a hand saw by the way) and gave them a semi-rounded front. At this point I had visions of my aquaplane going through the water like a rocket. Then I put the two planks together, put a piece of wood over the top to hold them side-by-side, and attached another piece of wood at the base. Of course, the two planks wouldn't fit together seamlessly, so Lee and I got some caulk and filled the space between them. When the aquaplane was finished, we put it in the water and off we went—at least ten feet, maybe fifteen—before the rope snapped. After about four ropes we finally got one that held.

I must have tried at least twenty-five times to get up on that "dumb aquaplane." In my frustration I was calling it dumb, although it had been my brilliant idea to begin with. When I finally *did* manage to ride on it, the water very quickly sprayed in-between the boards and right into my face. I had used non-waterproof caulking. I might have read that on the label, but I was in too much of a hurry to read instructions—another lesson learned through experience. Then I re-did the caulking, and finally it worked!

Lee and I learned through experiences like these that if there is a gap or an omission in an assignment, you find a way to fill in that gap—and that applied to schoolwork as well. When it came to academics, I was not the best student in the world. I had mostly A's and some B's, but I did only what it took to get by, and that approach was not acceptable to my parents. I remember one six-week term when I brought home a C in algebra. My dad said, "Okay, that's it. You are going to another school." The school he was referring to is a wonderful school today, but at the time, from my perspective, it was way too small—and more importantly, my friends were not there. I did *not* want to go. I cried and cried—deeply-felt, genuine tears. Dad finally relented, and gave me one more semester to pull up my grade. "If you don't," he said, "for your sake, you're going to have to transfer." Talk about motivation! I went to my wonderful teacher, got the help I needed, and received all A's for the rest of the year. As a result, I learned that asking for help when you need it is a smart move. I never had to go to "that other school," and I graduated with my friends.

Later, my brother Lee contracted meningitis, a serious inflammation of the membranes surrounding the brain and spinal cord. It was a very scary thing; Lee almost died when he was in high school. After he recovered, he had to go to "that other school"—the same one I'd had a fit about having to attend—to catch up academically, and he did beautifully! Lee persistently fought his way back from that disease, determined to excel in spite of his setback. Like our dad, my brother became a doctor—a very good one in heart, mind, and soul—serving others with a God-centered sense of purpose and excellence. Today he is an exceptional man in word and in deed. I am worried that if Lee reads these words of praise he might "get a big head," but in truth that would never happen. He's far too humble.

Lee nor I had ever heard of Calvin Coolidge's famous saying when we were learning to plow or to aquaplane or to work through academic challenges—but if we had, I'm certain we would have agreed with it. President Coolidge said:

> *Nothing in this world can take the place of persistence. Talent will not; nothing is more common than unsuccessful people with talent. Genius will not; unrewarded genius is almost a proverb. Education will not; the world is full of educated derelicts. Persistence and determination alone are omnipotent. The slogan "Press On!" has solved and always will solve the problems of the human race.*

HOUSEHOLD RULES AND WORDS TO LIVE BY

In our home we seldom ate supper without my dad being there; and since he was a doctor with a general practice, we never knew when he might get home. Later he would go back to study to become specialized in surgery, breaking the protocol of the day. But Dad was an innovator who truly felt it was the right thing to do, and doing the right thing was a cardinal rule in our house. My mother believed that waiting for Dad to come home for supper was the right thing to do, and, besides, we used that dinner time together to learn what each member of the family had done with the day's opportunities. If Dad wasn't home by eight o'clock we ate without him, but otherwise, we sat down at the table together and discussed the events of the day. *What did we do for someone else? Did we look for a need that was present and help if we could? What mistakes occurred, and how could we have handled them better?* I remember being so bored during many of those discussions, but now I realize their significance.

Much of our conversation centered on my dad's practice of medicine: what to do about this or that disease, how to prevent it, what foods were best from a nutritional standpoint to maintain health, and why that was important. We went over what had occurred in his medical world that day, and we couldn't help but learn a lot about the different medications and treatments being used. Fortunately, we didn't have television or video games to rush us away from the table, so we did a lot of family talking, played games, read books, or worked on some kind of project of my mother's design. I can testify to the truth of the adage that sometimes boredom begets creativity!

As I've said, Mother volunteered in almost every organization you could possibly imagine. She worked with her church, First Methodist of Houston, The Methodist Hospital, The Blue Bird Circle and the Texas Association of Hospitals and Homes (and its National Association as well.) She was a room mother and PTA volunteer for many years, and worked with Cub Scouts and Campfire Girls, too. I remember once, when her plate was especially full,

> **What did we do for someone else? Did we look for a need that was present and help if we could? What mistakes occurred, and how could we have handled them better?**

she told us, "If anyone asks for parent volunteers, I want you to *sit on your hands*. Do not raise them!" Mother had a leadership role in many of these organizations, and both of my parents were very active and highly respected in our community. We saw service demonstrated in their everyday life. In spite of the demands on her time, Mother was always there when we got home from school. Her family always came first. She was our kind, generous, and creative leader, modeling for us the Golden Rule she strived to live by: "Always do unto others as you would have them do unto you."

Learning in our family happened year-round, and not only at home and school. In the summertime our folks sent us to Cheley Colorado Camps outside of Estes Park—a place that had a major influence on my life. Cheley encouraged both interdependence and self-reliance, spurring campers to face new challenges and form strong relationships. The well-trained staff inspired trust, and made us eager to win their praise.

Cheley guided us daily in practicing the presence of God. Inspirational ideas and messages were not force-fed to us but were simply woven into the fabric of everyday life, and the camp staff made an effort in their actions, words, and deeds to promote positive values. Most of the walls around the camp bore inspiring mottoes that preached without pressure, leading us to think with every decision, "What would God want us to do?" I still remember many of the mottoes I learned at Cheley—things like, "So live that you could sell the family parrot to the town gossip," or "When you meet temptation, turn to the right." I was taught to learn from others who knew more than me, and I believe

> ## "So live that you could sell the family parrot to the town gossip."

I did. I learned I should "Never be afraid to try something new—because amateurs built the ark and professionals built the Titanic." These lessons still come to mind today. When I'm faced with a challenging situation I remember other mottoes like, "The dictionary is the only place where success comes before work," and that "Worry is like a rocking chair: it gives you something to do but doesn't get you anywhere." I learned so much in my summers there.

Perhaps Cheley first introduced me to the idea that worship was not confined to church, or only to Sunday. As I took in all of those wonderful words to live by, I was awakening to the true and living Word. My spiritual awareness came an inch at a time, but I thank God that it *did* come, and that He guided me to allow Him in. He was always there, of course, but I was not always aware of Him. He was knocking, but I hadn't yet opened the door.

I must have been about ten years old when I asked my Mother, "What is this Holy Ghost thing that they keep talking about in church?" She explained to me that the Holy Ghost—or the Holy Spirit—is "God's number one messenger," enabling us to experience His presence, and providing us the peace, joy, and hope that surpass all human understanding. I have since experienced His presence as an inner-guide telling me what is right and what is wrong—and prompting me to do things for other people that I would've never done on my own. I've come to understand that when people say, "God is talking to me," they are not having an ordinary conversation! God is not necessarily speaking, but He is sending a message. As it says in *The Little Prince*, "Sometimes what the heart sees is invisible to the eye."

While my Mother's explanation of the Holy Ghost was an eye-opener for me, the wonder of it rapidly gave way to other, more "visible" things. Even so, although I was mostly unaware of it happening, a door was opening in my life.

A BROADER EDUCATION

I was very fortunate in my education. The first part came courtesy of my parents, of course, and their school of "learning by doing." Then later, I had my experiences at Cheley Colorado Camps. After graduating from high school I enrolled at Southern Methodist University (SMU)—and many wonderful things happened there, too. I attended SMU during the "Doak Walker years" of the late 1940s. Walker's success (he was a three-time All-American and won the Heisman Trophy in 1948) made our campus quite an exciting place. There is nothing like a winning team to bond students on a campus, and recognition of the importance of bonding with colleagues was another learning experience for me.

> Recognition of the importance of bonding with colleagues was another learning experience for me.

I studied psychology in college at a time when experiential, hands-on learning was favored. One of my more memorable immersions into the field involved a short time of observation at a State Hospital that worked primarily with the mentally ill. While the hospital was using the best techniques available to it at the time, I must say that the treatments were very difficult to watch. Shock treatments were administered without anesthetic, straightjackets were used randomly, and over-medicating was the norm. As a young student there for observation and research, I was allowed to sit in occasionally on case reviews and treatments. What I witnessed there would, in time, become important in ways I could scarcely imagine.

In addition to experiences like these, I was required to take all sorts of "ridiculous" classes like math, government, history, religion and science. I fought it tooth-and-nail, but my advisor (who was the head of the Psychology Department) won out. I didn't see how these courses could possibly prepare me for a career, but I obeyed. In those days, you did what your elders told you to do! In one of these required classes (geology), I met my future husband, Dave. We've been married more than sixty-six years now, so I am very grateful for that "mean old" advisor!

A year or so before graduation, Dave and I had decided to get married. He wanted to go to law school, so I needed to work. He had served in WWII but the G.I. Bill didn't provide us with enough money to live on. This meant that by my senior year, I had some big decisions to make.

One of my psychology professors started talking to me and my fellow seniors about

> **Find the ember of God in each person you meet; and if you can, fan it into a fire.**

getting ready to go out into the work world. "Unless you're going on for a post-graduate degree," he said, "you'll have to get what you will need to be successful in another field. And the time to do so is *now.*"

Right then, I decided I'd better try to be a teacher. To do so I had to take thirty hours in a specific field (education) in order to become certified. And because of that "mean old advisor" who made me take all of those "dumb" required courses several semesters before, I was able to successfully fulfill the requirements for the teaching certificate in *one year.* I count this as one of God's many disguised miracles in my life. I may not have always known what I was doing, but *He* certainly had a plan!

My certification in education also required practice teaching, which seemed to me a waste of valuable time—after all, I was still majoring in "campusology" and enjoying it very much. But I got into practice teaching and absolutely loved it. I had a fabulous lead teacher, Miss McLemore.

I learned so much from her, especially in regards to observation. "Try to find the good in everybody," she instructed. So I became an observer of each and every student, seeking to find ways to help them succeed. She would often say, "Find the ember of God in each person you meet; and if you can, fan it into a fire."

In addition to these wonderful words of wisdom, Miss McLemore gave me a free hand in the classroom. At the time, I believed that she thought I was so good at teaching she could just let me take charge. I found out later that although she was a very fine teacher, she saw an opportunity to do something better with her time than stay in the classroom and supervise a rookie. She, too, was a proponent of experiential and consequential learning, giving me the opportunity to totally immerse myself in teaching methods that would prove invaluable in years to come. Leading my students in these tasks helped me become a better teacher because of the many opportunities to make mistakes. It's been said that if you fall on your face you are at least falling forward. If that is the case, I was *moving forward at a rapid rate.*

Looking back, I can see that my destiny—my role in the development of an interdependent, God-centered community based on mutual respect and work—was perhaps in God's sights from the very beginning. And in my life, I have seen that the experiential learning never stops. As He prepared me so many years ago, God is still in the process of equipping us for this Brookwood project. I have come to realize how He qualifies people—perhaps from early childhood—through a multitude of experiences, both good and bad. I love the expression, "God does not call the qualified, He qualifies the called." Today I see the diverse skills and passions developed through these experiences coming together at Brookwood in staff, donors, consultants, volunteers, prayer warriors, and everyone involved with the mission. Fortunately, He is not through with us yet.

Experiential learning never stops.

STORMS

By the late 1950s, Dave and I had three daughters and we were living in our first house on Holly Street in Bellaire, Texas: a little two-bedroom, one-bath bungalow on a big lot, near wonderful, caring neighbors. Ours was an old-fashioned kind of neighborhood where there were lots of children, not much TV, and plenty of outside play going on. Everyone's doors were open, and children were constantly moving in and out. Our young daughters, Vita, Vivian, and Vicki were in the thick of these neighborhood activities—following, watching, and play-acting with their friends. When the older girls put on productions, baby Vicki and our two cats were frequently dressed up to the nines, so that they could perform as well.

With two big sisters to emulate, Vicki was an early talker. I remember her first words when she was ten months old. We were going to California and we were driving because we didn't have the money for the five of us to go by train, much less by plane. It was a *very* long trip. After three days, we arrived in Arizona, preparing to go on to California, and Vicki had had enough. As I walked out from the motel holding her in my arms, she looked over and saw the car, and said clearly, and in protest, "Car-car. No."

> "Who but God would know that soon enough, the car would become our daughter's only place of comfort and solace?"

Dave and I were amazed. Looking back on those precious first words, I think, "Who but God would know that soon enough, the car would become our daughter's only place of comfort and solace?"

Just a few months later, on November 28, 1957, our family's world forever changed: Vicki had twenty-eight gran mal seizures that day. Any kind of seizure is traumatic for a child to experience or a parent to witness, but gran mal is the worst. A gran mal seizure is a devastating, total-body event, often causing the victim to lose consciousness for a period of time.

This lovable, adorable child was suffering horribly and so were we. To say that we were afraid is a serious understatement. We raced her that day to my dad, who was a doctor at Methodist Hospital, and he got in touch with a neurologist, who immediately admitted her to Methodist. We learned that Vicki had developed encephalitis and meningitis due to complications from the mumps, causing the seizures and resulting brain damage. She was immediately put on the anti-seizure medications of choice in those days—Dilantin and phenobarbital. The seizures stopped but she was over sedated. We decreased the dosage and the seizures continued at a lesser intensity for several days, then stopped for a time, maybe a day or two, before returning. My immediate reaction to this overwhelming situation was a tremendous desire to sleep, I suppose as a way to escape from a situation I believed I could not handle. I learned soon enough that running away from a problem is a race you never win.

Running away from a problem is a race you never win.

Vicki continued in this terrifying state for weeks—often seizing in gran mal form, and sometimes in a lesser form. The use of medications was not nearly so refined as it is today, but periodically she could get a few days of peace before the next series of seizures began. Her doctors were uncertain what medications should be used over an extended period of time, so we tried one drug and then another—but none of them were the answer. What we *didn't* know at the time was that the medications could and did cause tortuous pain, anxiety, fears, despondency, and all kinds of distressing behaviors. At times, we found nothing at all that could give her relief. It was truly a nightmare. This went on for about seven years until she was eight, and, all the while, we went from the hospital to home and back again and again.

My heart aches as I think back on that time. It was a terrible sort of hell, and I don't mean that in a profane way. The seizures continued and grew less frequent, but, as I said, the medications meant to help Vicki caused her harm as well. It was, to us, a no-win situation.

During the worst times, Vicki screamed, hit, and bit herself, and she exhibited many variations of self-abusive behavior. In general, she was uncontrollable. She stopped eating and would not sleep until she quite literally passed out from exhaustion. Many times she went without sleep for two or three days, during which she was in a state of constant turmoil.

Our daughter would live on death's door at the hospital for weeks; then we would be able to bring her home for a few weeks, before we'd end up having to take her back to the hospital again.

The doctors, who by this time had called in second and third opinions, would eventually throw up their hands and ask us, "What do you think?" or, "What do you want us to do?" They, too, were at their wits' end. I understood, but I didn't want to be asked what I thought or what we ought to do. I wanted someone in authority to say, "I have the solution, and this is what we're *going* to do."

It wasn't that we didn't have good doctors; it was just that at that time there simply were no proven answers. We had consulted the best medical minds available, and there was nothing *anyone* could do.

During these dark days I instinctively turned to God and begged for His help. When no dramatic, immediate, positive action came, I'm afraid I took that as a refusal. In reality, however, He was saying to me, *"Take my hand, walk with me and trust."*

Take my hand, walk with me and *trust*.

WHAT NEXT?

This roller coaster of seizures, relative calm, more seizures and hospitalizations continued for several years. When Vicki was around three, a pediatric neurologist advised us that she would never speak and never recognize us; and if she survived past childhood, she would live on the very edges of life. When the seizures stopped for a period of time at age eight, Vicki was doing *nothing*. She seemed to hear nothing, see nothing, feel nothing. If we put her down on the floor and didn't move her, she'd be there until we did move her. We were told repeatedly that we should put her away, because if we didn't, she would ruin our family.

Although we had begun to ask ourselves what kind of life we could give Vicki if she was not going to get *well*, we could not imagine "putting her away." Some folks *are* able to place their child elsewhere, a choice that

may well be right for their situation. But even though Vicki was functioning at an extremely low level, we decided not to go that route. We were
hoping against hope to *find another way.*

Although we didn't know it then, I realize now that part of the answer
had been shown to me during my time at SMU. I remembered my experience at the State Hospital, where the old methods of dealing with the mentally retarded and the mentally ill had been so disturbing to me. Although
those methods were going out of practice when I was told to put Vicki
away, the images remained in my mind. There was simply no way that
I was going to subject my daughter to a situation like that—even though
I knew that what I had witnessed was no longer common practice. Back
then certain classifications like "moron," "idiot," and "imbecile" were
actually used when referring to the intellectual level of the "retarded." I
didn't like those words, I didn't like the prevalent attitude, and I just didn't
want that kind of environment for Vicki.

It's hard to believe today, but once upon a time, most people that were
different from what was considered the norm—either physically or mentally—were routinely shunned, laughed at, and ridiculed—and in some
backward places even tortured or used for experimental research. Thank
God perceptions have changed radically from what they once were, even
up to the middle of the twentieth century.

Just fifty or sixty years ago, when we were faced with making decisions
about Vicki's future, people like her were, in some cases, being viewed as
waste products. Today they've been given a whole new chance at life from a
different angle. Our family needed to live this reality to really understand it—
and God's will for us was to work along with Him to gain that perspective.
Although we did not recognize it at the time, to us the first step in improving
Vicki's life was keeping her at home, no matter what others told us.

ANGELS ALL AROUND US

In addition to what this challenge was doing to Vicki, it also took its toll on us, and on my parents who lived nearby. Fortunately, Vita and Vivian were doing well in our wonderful neighborhood, and they had tremendous family support. Through the first eight years of Vicki's life, Dave, my mother, and I spent a lot of our time at the hospital. Dave and I took turns, and we practically wore out the pavement on Holcombe/Bellaire Boulevard going to and from the Texas Medical Center to be with Vicki, then back home to be with Vita and Vivian.

In those days, Dave was working for the Scurlock Oil Company, and they were fantastic about encouraging him to put his family first. Mr. Scurlock and his son-in-law Jack Blanton provided the time and flexibility that enabled us to care for Vicki the best way we knew how. Dave would come to the hospital after work and stay a few hours with me while I would sleep. Then he would awaken me about 2 a.m., go home and get a few hours sleep himself before going back to work. It was very difficult for him, but he never complained or shirked his obligation to the family as a whole. He and I usually managed between us to be at home with the girls for several hours each day.

They put their love into practice, day in and day out.

Vicki would often be in the hospital for weeks at a time, all the while with us thinking that this day might be her last. When Dave and I were both with her, my parents and an angel neighbor, Jean Farge, helped us care for Vita and Vivian. The girls were moving rapidly through childhood, growing up in a most unusual situation. They both have become outstanding, faith-filled adults, demonstrating great energy, purpose, and service for others. I credit a lot of that to Mother, Dad, and Jean, who did more than care—they put their love into practice, day in and day out.

We had many sleepless nights—hundreds, I'd venture to say. Friends, neighbors, family, and doctors would tell us, "You are both going to collapse from this strain—you must stop, you simply can't keep this up." But, somehow, we didn't skip a beat. We received the energy needed to carry on from what was at that time in our lives, an "unidentified source." On several occasions we would respond to the people who cautioned us and say, "You know what? *We* are amazed that we are not wiped out, but we aren't, and we don't know why." That unidentified source was our unlimited filling station. Of course today we recognize that it was God who sustained us. He had to knock down barriers time and again to get through to us, but, even so, we received His grace.

There were many times that the only peace Vicki could get came from riding in the car, hour upon hour. Dave and I took turns day and night, driving her around. My fantastic parents did, too. One night, at about 3:30 a.m., I was driving Vicki to calm her. A car pulled into the intersection in front of us and stopped at a diagonal, blocking the street. A man got out and pulled his coat away from his body, and I saw that he had a gun. All I could think to ask God was that if this man was going to shoot, to please let him shoot both of us.

He came to the door on my side, and I lowered the window. He said he was a deputy sheriff. And then he said, "I've watched you drive around this neighborhood night after night, and I want to know if I can help." I explained about our most unusual patterns and why we were doing what we were doing. He showed me where he lived, and he said to please call on him at *any* time. What a very nice man—-and how good it was to know that someone else—someone we'd never met—was willing to share our journey, even in a small way.

> What a blessing it was to ride on His back instead of questioning every move.

There must have been hundreds of similar events, maybe not as dramatic, but all evidencing the caring and contributing neighbors, friends, and family who surrounded us. At that point, I certainly believed in God, although mostly subconsciously. I think Dave and I could both feel the extraordinary strength that was keeping us more focused on "how-to" than "why us?" What a blessing it was to ride on His back instead of questioning every move. We lived scared and desperate, afraid we were going to lose Vicki. But miraculously, we kept moving forward. Later, I sometimes used to wonder: was that stupidity? Or a lack of realization of the seriousness of the situation? I believe now it was neither; but instead, an inherent, childlike trust in God. Somehow our refusal to put Vicki away did *not* ruin our family. Instead, I think it did the opposite—it provided a fertile ground for God to work. Our girls saw the unification of family and the tremendous outpouring of love and dedication from extended family and friends. And as a result, they grew up wanting to serve others.

L A U G H T E R   R I S I N G

I believe it was humorist Erma Bombeck who said, "Laughter rises out of tragedy when you need it most, and rewards you for your courage." Those early years were a blur of emotions, but they were not without moments of laughter. Vita and Vivian became adept at adjusting to the stares and questions of other people when Vicki pulled one of what we called her "stunts." While of course she could not control them, those stunts usually involved screaming and yelling, flailing around, or pounding on something. Fortunately she never hit people. Vita and Vivian quickly figured out how to deflect attention from these behaviors when we were in public. For example, if Vicki let out a blood-curdling scream while standing in line at the cafeteria, everyone would look around in the direction of the scream. The girls would look over Vicki's head, too, as if they were also trying to identify the screamer—and it usually worked.

At the pool, Vicki swam in the most unorthodox way imaginable. She learned to love the water at Lucy and A. J. Foyt's pool across the street from our house. We had that pool to ourselves most every day, but every once in a while we would take her to a private club pool. When we did, other children often laughed and giggled and made comments about "that weirdo." It embarrassed Vita and Vivian—and me—but they figured it out pretty quickly. They would brush off the unkindness by saying that Vicki was choreographing a new synchronized swimming routine for the Olympics. Once that comment broke the ice with the other children, they would simply explain Vicki's condition and brag on her ability to swim as well in *her* way as they could in theirs. They felt good about teaching others, about protecting their sister and—to be honest—about putting

The Streit family during a lull in Vicki's illness.
(Left to right) Yvonne, Vivian, Dave, Vita, and Vicki in front.

> **It was one of the first dynamic, recognizable God-nudges that I would get along the way.**

those who spoke unkind words in their place.

Most of the children in our own neighborhood had been told about Vicki's brain injury, and they tolerated her mostly by ignoring her. Quite simply, they didn't know how to respond. However, the boy who was the neighborhood leader (today he would probably be called a bully) cruelly made fun of Vicki. One day I heard him ridiculing her, and that just about did me in. I took Vicki into the house of my friend, and I charged out to get this kid. I was going to *level* him. Heading down the street to do just that, I got to the edge of his driveway when I received a strong *nudge*. It was one of the first dynamic, recognizable God-nudges that I would get along the way, and I would eventually get many. With that nudge, and in a split second, I did a 180-degree turn in my approach.

The nudge pushed me to make this boy Vicki's friend, to explain to him what happened to her when she was just a year old, how we loved her, and how she needed people to be her champions and to watch over her. And, as God would have it, the bully did become her champion, and the whole neighborhood followed his example.

Somehow, with God's help, good neighbors, and a strong sense of humor, we got through those early years—but not without making our share of mistakes and learning some very valuable lessons. Our love for our children increased, and so did the desire to do something to make Vicki's life more livable. Thankfully, I learned not to fear my own mistakes. You probably don't know anyone who has made as many mistakes as I have. But those failures have led to successes in ways I could never have foreseen. In fact, I've come to believe that failure is sometimes God's way of saying, "Try another way". I think my Mother would be tickled that He agrees with her.

Failure is sometimes God's way of saying, "Try another way."

"WE'RE ALL OKAY."

By 1964, Vicki was well into her eighth year. Her seizures were mostly controlled, and the side effects of the medications used to treat her were at least manageable. I had gone all over the country—Missouri, Pennsylvania, Delaware, Rhode Island, Washington D. C., Illinois, Indiana, Florida, California—talking to anyone and everyone who might offer hope of a cure for our youngest daughter. Remembering that Vicki had become sick overnight, I *continued* to cling to the hope that she could get well overnight. We investigated anything and everything that might provide the miracle cure we longed for.

One day my good friend Katie Harrop encouraged me to go and hear Dr. Newell Kephart, a psychology and education professor from Purdue University, who was speaking in Houston. Even though Dr. Kephart was a noted expert in diagnosing and treating slow-learning, learning disabled and brain-damaged children—I didn't want to go. I didn't want to face another dead end, and I certainly didn't want someone to tell me *again* to put Vicki away. I made some rather lame excuse to Katie. Then I got another nudge for which I am eternally gratefully—so I went.

"How do we teach so that the student will be successful?"

Looking back I consider going to hear Dr. Kephart's speech that day to be a major, pivotal point in our family's story and in the Brookwood story. He was simply amazing. He demonstrated that rare quality of common sense, coupled with the sort of compassion, determination, and creativity that unlocks doors and offers opportunity. He accepted children like Vicki just as they were—disabilities and all; and he made no pretense of trying to make them "normal." His attitude reminded me of a sermon I'd heard soon after the book *I'm OK, You're OK* came out. The minister commented on its title and said that he had a more appropriate title and suggested, "I'm *not* OK, you're *not* OK, but *that's* OK." Dr. Kephart recognized that even though these children were *not* "OK" from a human standpoint, they *were* "OK" from a spiritual standpoint. He wanted to start where the children were and help them have the fullest life possible, not denying their disabilities but embracing them.

Slowly and surely, Dave and I came to accept that Vicki was going to remain severely brain-injured. Dr. Kephart's teaching awakened us to that fact, but also to the idea that that there were still things that could be done to help her have a better life. He felt strongly that the training he and his team developed could help kids with disabilities learn to, as he said, "play with the cards they'd been dealt" and adapt to their unique situations.

On that day, although I didn't know it at the time, Dr. Newell Kephart became my chief mentor in education. He impressed me with his approach of identifying what type of education process would be most beneficial to a particular individual and asking, "How do we teach so that the student will be successful?" As I listened, I became increasingly aware of the tremendous importance of observation—a powerful teaching tool that would one day become a critical part of Brookwood's success.

Immediately following Dr. Kephart's presentation, I made my way over to thank him for his words. He was a nice-looking, athletic man, probably in his early fifties, dressed in a coat and tie and brimming with kindness and confidence. As he inquired about my interest in his subject, his manner

> **"God already has children like Vicki in a very special section in His Kingdom—but He wants us to enjoy them as much as He does."**

immediately put me at ease. I told him about Vicki—adding that she was severely brain-damaged, and that I didn't think she would be a candidate for his program.

"That's where you're wrong," he replied. "This is the very type of child that we love to work with. Our goal is to take them out of a state of nothingness and give them the opportunity to become a part of their world—*and* to help their parents and others learn to communicate in whatever way works for them."

"You see," he added, "God already has children like Vicki in a very special section in His Kingdom—but He wants us to enjoy them as much as He does."

His message was disarmingly honest—no one was going to make Vicki well—but it was also affirming: he did not at all view her as "damaged goods." I could tell that he believed he could help us—and that he wanted to try. Dr. Kephart invited me to bring Vicki to Purdue University in Indiana to see if we could teach her to "play with the cards she'd been dealt."

As positive as all of this sounded, I was very apprehensive about taking such a major step. So many of the steps that I had already taken had turned out to be of little or no value. The old saying "Nothing ventured; nothing gained" occurred to me, but I was certainly not eager to take this very fragile child across the country to a program that I didn't know that much about.

I went home after the talk and told my family about what I had learned. We visited about it for what seemed like a long time. Vita and Vivian were ten and nine by this time, and they wanted us to do anything that would help Vicki. I was very proud of them, and their encouragement was wonderful, but the one who really pushed me into going up to observe Dr. Kephart's program in action was my mother.

It was January, and the weather was awful. I hated the thought of the long drive, and had half-convinced myself it was probably going to be a wild goose chase anyway. In other words, I was talking myself out of going all the way up to West Lafayette, Indiana. Mother and I must have weighed the pros and cons of this venture for days. She and Dave were the only people who truly understood how difficult a trip like that would be with Vicki if we decided to take her, and Mother had the same reservations, apprehensions, and fears that I had.

I remember Mother saying that if we went

This new outlook was emerging.

and it was useless, that was okay; but if we didn't go and at least *listen* and *try*, that was not okay. Finally she said to me, "I need to ask you a question Yvonne: If *you* don't do something, just who do you think will?" Being sufficiently challenged, off I went to Indiana with my friend Katie—without our children—to investigate this program first-hand. Katie, who also had an involved daughter, was eager to make the trip.

I was right about the weather but wrong about the other excuses I had conjured up. I saw that Dr. Kephart and his staff really practiced what they preached. I was beyond thrilled to find that they really *wanted* to work with children like Vicki. I knew that they didn't make any money in this endeavor, so I could see that his invitation was made from a sincere desire to help us and other families like ours. The experience was a wonderful eye-opener, and Katie and I both felt that through this Purdue program, we could possibly provide better lives for our children. My old attitude had been that in order for Vicki to have a meaningful life we had to "make her well." My new attitude was a strong desire for Vicki to be content, at peace, *and loved*. This new outlook was emerging. Dr. Kephart's program offered promise toward that goal.

Back I came to Houston. I discussed the idea of taking Vicki up to Purdue with Dave and my parents. All of us agreed we should do this, and then I got cold feet *again*. It was crazy to go to Indiana in the winter. (Same song, second verse.) Where would we stay? What exactly would we get out of the program? Vicki was too damaged despite Dr. Kephart's encouragement to the contrary, and it just wouldn't do any good. Mostly I was scared—and the person who is afraid has two choices: Forget everything and run, or face everything and rise. And so finally, with prayer and encouragement from my parents, Dave, Vicki, and I went off to Purdue.

Once we arrived, Dr. Kephart interviewed Dave and me separately and in depth. One of the most important questions he asked was, "What does your daughter respond to?"My answer was very simple. "Nothing." "Well," he said, "She responds to something, and we have to find out what it is. That will be my first goal tomorrow morning. I have an idea, but we will have to have the class meet in the gym instead of the classroom."

The next day Dr. Kephart asked the class to move to the gymnasium where he could easily address all of the families who had come from throughout the U.S. to learn. He laid our eight-year-old, Vicki, on the trampoline and stood beside it, pushing on the mat, bouncing her very gently. He did this for about an hour and fifteen minutes as he lectured, then we broke for a mid-morning snack. I took Vicki, changed her diapers, gave her a snack, and put her back on the trampoline.

Dr. Kephart returned to the class, but moved to stand on the other side of the trampoline, explaining that his arm was getting very tired. Once again, this master of multi-tasking started bouncing Vicki while he lectured to the class, and did so until we broke for lunch at 11:45. When he stopped, Vicki went "Uhhh. Uhhhh. Uhhhhh."

She had responded! Through my tears I heard Dr. Kephart say, "Aha! Now we have a key to that hidden treasure within. It is *movement.* We have something we can use as a reward, a motivator, to get Vicki's attention—so we must train her to *want* attention. Our goal will be to teach her to respond by using a movement-related reward or consequence."

> ## Now we have a key to that hidden treasure within.

Then we began experimenting with "desirable" consequences—a desk chair that twirled around, or a bite of food that she really liked. We presented a learning task designed to get her to "attend" (pay attention and receive information) and respond (take an action of some sort). The idea was to entice her to pay attention and then reinforce that "attending" with a reward, a desired consequence.

> ## The power of *observation* is uppermost in the hierarchy of determining how someone effectively learns.

This practice began a series of motivational movements that we used for years. We tried twirling Vicki in a desk chair and wore several of those out. We swung her by her arms,—and yes, we knew that this wasn't particularly good for her; but when you have a child who has never requested *anything,* and she shows a desire for something, you take liberties that you wouldn't ordinarily take. We even rode a tandem bicycle. In short, we did anything we could that created motion and seemed to interest her.

Dr. Kephart then began to teach me how to teach her to learn. The first thing that he emphasized was that "the power of *observation* is uppermost in the hierarchy of determining how someone effectively learns." He had already determined through observation that Vicki's best avenue of learning was through tactile motor stimulation.

In order to teach her to attend and respond we needed to have a task for her to do. Knowing this, Dr. Kephart taught me to put my hand over her hand and grasp a pencil—or any object—with my hand still over hers, actually doing the motion as if we were one. Once we managed the grasp, I needed to teach her to release, prying her fingers away from the object one at a time. Then we graduated to a series of movements: grasp, lift, place, and release. After what seemed like a few million tries at this prescribed procedure, I could begin to move my hand toward hers, and that signal got her started. She would complete the task. Then I could couple commands with movement, saying the word "grasp" and moving my hand toward hers until the desired action took place. The next step was to not move my hand toward her at all, but to simply say the word "grasp." The progression went from concentrating on tactile-motor instruction to tactile-motor-visual instruction, then to eliminating the tactile-motor and relying on visual only, and finally to eliminating the visual and injecting auditory. Vicki did not distinguish each word per se, but she could "translate" the tone and sound of my voice as I spoke the word and then follow the "command."

Now, when the component parts of the task are presented, she does them without prompts. This teaching technique is called a "fading procedure." You begin with the most easily received sensory input and progress to the weaker stimuli until the desired goal can be instigated through minimal sensory input. In other words, through repetition you "fade" the more intense sensory input methods to the less intense ones.

Dr. Kephart was a great proponent of the ABC (Antecedent-Behavior-Consequence) method of teaching that intentionally utilizes the observable behavior techniques that almost any child exhibits. Is she paying more attention to sounds? Or to sights? Or to touch? Or to movement? These tools may be used to strengthen her asset avenues of learning, while also strengthening the deficit avenues

> **Students must be taught to enjoy the sensation of accomplishment.**

of learning. Does the child receive words as meaningful? Or do the words or their sounds distract her from the task you've set up? Is it preferable to teach in a room with no visual clutter, which could be a detractor? Or is she able to disregard the excess visual stimuli? Observing a child in ordinary, everyday situations can offer clues as to what level of distractions he/she may be encountering.

During this period of time I met and worked with Sheila Doran-Benyon, a protégé of Dr. Kephart, and she became a lifelong friend and colleague. Sheila was working with a group of children with special needs at St. Francis Day School; and, as a volunteer there, I encountered many levels and varieties of disabilities that would be an invaluable help to me in my eventual work with the students at Briarwood and the citizens of Brookwood.

For example, attending (paying attention) and responding to instruction was important to parents and teachers, no matter what level of disability they were encountering. If you can't get a child to "pay attention" her chances of learning are decreased. Because I was able to observe these varying teaching techniques that were being tried with *and* without success, I was far better equipped to determine the most effective teaching methods for children with varying disabilities. Working with Sheila was a meaningful continuation of my indoctrination and studies at Purdue.

As I was first learning these techniques from Dr. Kephart, Vicki was functioning at a level too low for effective visual/auditory observation; therefore, we used a tactile/motor procedure—the grasp-and-release technique of hand-over-hand that I described—in order to teach her. The idea was to accomplish something—*anything*—and then work toward the completion of an assigned task, which would hopefully provide a sense of accomplishment. This feeling doesn't just happen, however; students must be taught to enjoy the sensation of accomplishment. If they get this feeling often enough, it probably will ultimately provide such enjoyment or fulfillment that they begin to seek it again and again.

Dr. Kephart also wisely reminded me that I was a mother first, and a teacher second. In order to help Vicki differentiate who I was at a given time, he explained that we should set a space aside for her training *only*. For our home program, he suggested that I arrange a little table and two chairs in a room that she did not use. He also told me that I needed to put on a smock when I became the teacher and that I should also put on a different demeanor. I was to take the smock off when the session was over, once again becoming "mother." In his work with Vicki he had found that talk or noise of any kind tended to distract her, so I was not to talk unnecessarily. In addition, Vicki should sit at a table facing a blank wall so that she would be more likely to pay attention to me as I instructed her; I was to be sitting on the same level as she was.

I decided that as Vicki's teacher I would wear a red smock. When we began each learning session, I would put on my red smock, situate Vicki in her "classroom" and work with her for about twenty or thirty minutes, or until I recognized that she was zoning out. Then I would call it quits when *I* felt that we should stop, instead of letting her dictate when to stop. By doing this, I could maintain control of the session. Before too long, she began to enjoy our sessions so much that she would actually get my smock and bring it to me!

We continued on the grasp-and-release task with the hand-over-hand technique until I was able to just move my hand toward her, and then use only the visual prompt. We had finally progressed to the point where she could pick up the pencil or object, put it on a target, and let go. I had no way of knowing it at the time, but this procedure would become the predecessor to Vicki placing 11,000 small pots into flats at the Brookwood horticulture center in later years. She was very proud of her accomplishment in her own way, and I can assure you I was also proud of her.

At this point, these lessons were only baby steps, but Vicki was emerging out of nothingness.

Vicki was emerging out of nothingness.

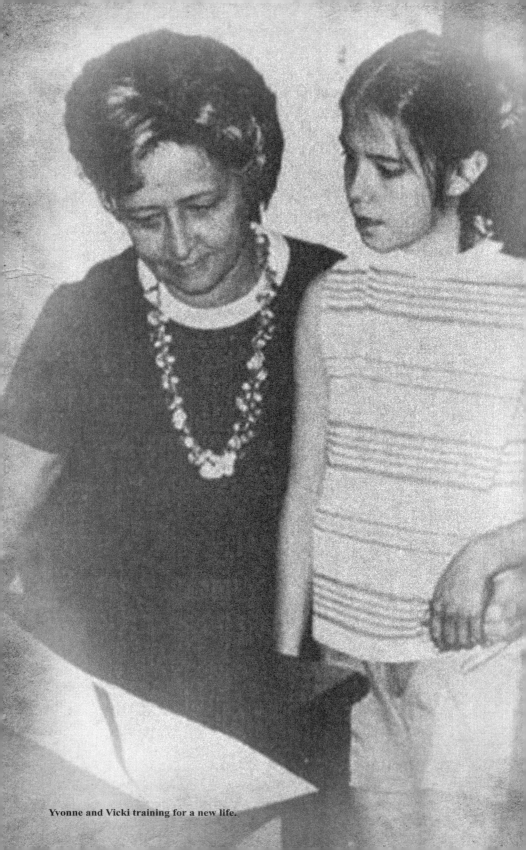

Yvonne and Vicki training for a new life.

II.

S P R O U T S

This need to help Vicki was growing into something bigger. The seed was planted in the ground of our ordinary family, no different than many other families. It was nurtured by the lessons I learned from my parents and grandparents, the wisdom of the mentors Dave and I found near and far, our own stubborn selfishness, and a blessed lack of understanding of just how big this challenge we faced really was.

At every critical juncture, first in caring for Vicki and then on the path to what would become Brookwood, God showed us what we needed to do next. He poured His wisdom onto the situation and something bigger and more beautiful than we had ever imagined began to grow. As we slowly began to realize just how present God was in our struggles, we became more and more excited to see His hand at work. Who knows how we might have reacted if He had shown us at the beginning what He was asking us to help Him create? Instead, he gave us little seeds, we learned how to nurture them, and slowly over time, the sprouts began to grow.

As we slowly began to realize just how present God was in our struggles, we became more and more excited to see His hand at work.

SHARING THE LEARNING

I had been very fortunate to be able to find and deeply study various programs that might help Vicki. In addition to my trips to Purdue, I attended similar seminars at UCLA and USC. I was able observe and participate in Dr. Ivar Lovaas' work at UCLA with the autistic and the work at USC regarding the response of the autistic to command cues. While all this travel and study was giving me plenty of ammunition for creative teaching, my lawyer husband was the real hero. He was working full time at Scurlock Oil and guiding Vicki in her exercises and with patterning at home. Dave was a great dad to our girls even though he lived in a state of exhaustion, and we were both learning—from that expert named experience and from Vicki—that change, failure, and perseverance are not four-letter words, and together they can be the gateway to success.

When we returned from Purdue in the mid-sixties, I had Vicki at a local day program for children with special needs. They had a very caring program, but a number of my fellow parents and I, although we really appreciated the work these people did, wanted more—more stimulation, more life skills training and development, and more opportunities for our children. We tried to persuade some of the public school districts to develop a program utilizing the methods we had discovered at UCLA and Purdue; but the need for change was perceived as an obstacle, and so it didn't happen.

When no other avenue opened up to our group, I began working with children in my backyard in 1965. I'm often asked, "How did these people find out about what you were doing?" The answer to that is that if you find your child in a desperate situation, you actively seek out information or people who may be able to help. Maybe you run into them at church or at the grocery store, or a neighbor may know of someone who knows someone. In a very short period of time, more children came to us whose parents were in the same boat, hoping to get some sort of help in order to improve their children's lives.

We soon ran out of room, but fortunately, not out of willing helpers. Our friend Ginny Rorschach, who helped in the development of this program from the time it was in our backyard, also helped with the patterning program purported to help rehabilitate areas of the brain that were neuro-logically impaired. Other friends, neighbors, and family members regular-ly came to our house to help put Vicki through a series of exercises for this program, one of several programs that I researched and tried in order to make Vicki "well." These programs provided Vicki a lot of attention, and she was a fantastically good "guinea pig" but only a few parts of them did what they were touted to do.

Friends also helped us construct an obstacle course with tubes, ladders, saw horses, a trampoline, and a balance beam in our yard and provided other play and "therapy" supplies. I remember all these volunteers with deep gratitude because I *know* how inconvenient it became for them to be at our house at a certain time on a certain day week after week in addi-tion to their very busy schedules. These angels, disguised as people, truly blessed our lives.

These angels, disguised as people, truly blessed our lives.

When I realized that we had outgrown our backyard I first thought we had better just call a halt to this idea. What on earth was I trying to do anyway? The answer that came to me was that I had had the opportunity to see some wonderful educational ideas, and they were not going to be introduced to this group of children if I didn't share them. Then I thought, "Who am I that I should keep this all to myself?"

Feeling another big nudge, I began searching for a place where we could meet and work with children with similar needs. I had discovered that public schools offered very little in the way of special education, so I must have gone to twenty churches in our area, explaining over and over again the tremendous need. I did not receive interest from any of them. By the latter part of 1966, it truly seemed that it was time to throw in the towel. Then Sally Woolrich, the principal at St. Francis Day School, encour-aged me—another nudge—to talk to the minister at the church next door to St. Francis, Memorial Drive Baptist. The senior minister was on sabbat-ical so I spoke with the assistant minister, a man by the name of David

Humphrey. Pastor Humphrey said that we could use some of their class-rooms *if* we would leave them clean and not disturb any of their supplies. We jumped on this opportunity like a duck on a June bug, and we began.

The children I had been working with in our backyard came to this new location, but there was another obstacle. I had not yet learned how to vary the teaching content or method so that I could include Vicki, who was not capable of participating in this semi-group setting, and I really didn't have anybody to help me with her. Ginny came to my aid again, saying, "Well, I can help, and I want to help. I can't do anything with the others, but I can take care of Vicki while you work with these other children." That was one of the many seeds Ginny would sow.

A few weeks later, I was outside at Memorial Drive Baptist Church working with some of the kids and a woman I'd never seen before walked by. She came over and introduced herself, and said, "My name is Ann Schomberg, and I live in that house right over there. I'm a physical thera-pist, and I wondered if I could help you."

I said, "Well, that'd be wonderful, but there's no pay in it. Nothing. No one pays to come, and no one gets paid to work."

She said, "Oh, I don't care. I'm not looking for money. I'm looking for a place where I could help." All I could think to say was, "You have certainly come to the right place!" I was ec-static to get the help, and Ann was a super-star—a knowledgeable

Creating situations where the proper response was demanded.

spark plug of positive energy. She walked right in, contributed beautifully, and never missed a beat. She also had a seed to sow.

A few months later, another lady came by, and said, "I have a degree in art therapy, and I wonder if I could help." Her name was Rosemary Larson, and she explained that she had a son who needed our kind of program. "Could you use me?" she asked. It took about a fraction of a second to say yes. Rosemary was an outstanding teacher, and we became exceptionally good friends and colleagues in developing Briarwood and Brookwood.

So, with Ann's and Rosemary's skills added to my research and ex-perience, we were up and running. Our program, based on Dr. Kephart's book *Success Through Play*, wove appropriate academics into a play-type setting to develop effective teaching methods, such as creating situations where the proper response was demanded. We follow that same process at Brookwood to this day.

During our time at Memorial Drive Baptist we "accidentally" transitioned in our developing program from focusing on just children with functional disabilities to another type of child with different challenges. Persons with functional disabilities cannot function comfortably in society, as we know it today. No one had a name or a category for these other children at the time (they later became known as the learning disabled), but they were responding *dramatically* to the philosophy and techniques that were used at Purdue. As we and the rest of the world became more aware of how to best serve these two different student populations, Briarwood and Brookwood would eventually provide for their different needs; but for now, we were all learning together.

We felt we were making some real progress when the senior minister of the church came back from sabbatical and decided that our activities were encroaching on their Sunday School program. He thought it might be a good idea for us to leave, and I certainly understood his concerns and the decision. The church had been wonderful to us, and we owed them a debt of gratitude. But once again, same song, seventeenth verse: our unorthodox school was searching for a home.

NEXT STEPS

Not long after we learned we would be leaving Memorial Drive Baptist, I approached Bobbi Reed, who had a day care/pre-school center, Le Petite Preschool and Nursery, and asked if she would let us use a part of their facilities to work with our children with special needs. She was delighted to have us.

We left Memorial Drive Baptist and went to the wonderful Le Petite location. There, we used methods developed from a Pennsylvania program called the Neurological Institute for the Achievement of Human Potential that included patterning and dietary supplements. We also included operant conditioning techniques from UCLA and, of course, the Purdue program—as well as any other method we discovered that just might help our children.

The combination of these elements provided a very effective way of getting and maintaining our students' attention. In the operant conditioning program, for example, an instructor would give a command visually, orally or with any sensory input method that worked. When the child performed the task, she would be rewarded with a bite of food. This was usually done at mealtime, and it was very effective at getting and keeping the child's attention; as well as getting her to cooperate by doing the targeted task.

During this "try anything" period we discarded some of the ideas we had picked up in our travels, but the ones from Purdue and UCLA remained. The time we spent at Le Petite Nursery School refined our methodology, but in time some of the parents of the normally-abled children at the center complained. They feared our group would somehow "infect" their children with abnormalities, and I understood their concerns. Their feelings were quite prevalent at the time, and so our wonderful friend Bobbi Reed had to ask us to leave. She did this through tears, because she loved our kids. Bobbi was a true good Samaritan who helped us when we were being shunned by other facilities, but she finally had to give in to the wishes of the majority students' parents in order to save her school. We were discouraged, of course, but I've come to understand that "being defeated is often a temporary condition; giving up is what makes it permanent." None of us were ready for that!

BACK ON THE STREET

Once again we had no place to meet, this time with twenty or more children and their parents. I went from door to door, school to school, and church to church trying to find another setting that we could use, but we were met with much skepticism. Public school programs devoted to working with the "retarded" were quite limited. Those few that did exist were under resourced, and the waiting time to get into them could be years, not months. Where could we go, I wondered? I didn't know, but I couldn't stop looking.

I found a school program in another Houston church and asked them if we could join them. They said yes, so we packed up and moved again, continuing to use the methods that were making such a difference for our children. Still, we were not following the traditional school curriculum. Our program was based on movement: fitness and play to stimulate their interest and cause them to attend and respond. Once they did, we were able to integrate reading, writing, and arithmetic when appropriate, through play, which offered a non-threatening and effective way of presenting academics.

So many of our challenged children were sedentary because they lacked the ability to participate in normal everyday activities because their motor abilities were inadequate. They were weak, had poor balance, were unsure of their ability to walk or throw a ball, and therefore were unable to explore their environment or take advantage of experiential learning through daily living. We used play, marching, singing, exploring, scavenger hunts, and the old reliable obstacle course—to provide a helpful and healthful foundation for developing fitness and "opening the door" for all types of learning. These activities increased and strengthened their muscle tone and instilled the self-confidence they needed to walk or run or to maintain balance. By making mistakes, our students learned not to fear them and instead realized that mistakes are a part of learning.

> **"Being defeated is often a temporary condition; giving up is what makes it permanent."**

Additionally, by presenting academic skill development through enjoyable activities and removing failure opportunities, we smoothed the road to success. Over time these activities allowed the students to emerge into a happier, more contented life—a life in which they were able to handle their disabilities as well as possible. We kept data on what they were able to do when they started an activity and the progress they were making over a period of time. They were shown their accomplishments, and their confidence and self-esteem grew even beyond their own initial expectations.

Not surprisingly, however, these new approaches to learning were not accepted at that church's school, either. The other teachers thought our abandonment of the "standard curriculum" was almost sacrilegious. One concerned father told me his son was actually looking forward to coming to school, and therefore he must not be learning anything; and, once again, we were asked to take our "wonderful" program somewhere else.

It's hard to convey how truly devastating these failures were; but we went on, and those wonderful, strength-giving nudges kept coming. By this time, I had convinced myself that in order to undertake a mission like ours, it really helps when God

> **By making mistakes, our students learned not to fear them.**

sets you up to be a little dumb, a little naïve, a little hard-headed, very competitive, and in a lot of need!

After another search, we found the welcome mat out for us at St. Philip Presbyterian Church, not far from Houston's Galleria. By now we had almost fifty students, and we hired a salaried teacher for the first time. Her name was Peggy Brown, and she was one of the best teachers I have been fortunate enough to work with. Peggy stayed with us as a teacher during our formative years. Then, she must have realized that she could not make a living on the pittance my husband was paying her, so she had to leave us. She is now Peggy McGaughy, one of Houston's leading interior designers, and she continues to be very influential as a member of our Board of Directors. Peggy was a gift from God to us, and we were grateful for the seeds she sowed then and continues to sow today.

When St. Philip's agreed to let us use their facilities, they put a restriction on the agreement: we would have to have our own facilities after three years. At the time, I didn't think this was very nice, but I later realized this was another God nudge, signaling us to get with it and build in order to touch the lives of far more children than we could have if we stayed at the church.

At St. Philip's, the uncategorized students who had difficulty learning from traditional methods and who so positively responded to our methods were fast becoming the majority. We had started the school for children like Vicki who had functional disabilities, individuals who cannot function comfortably in society, as we know it today. The children who were rapidly increasing our enrollment were those who were simply having trouble in a regular classroom. They were the class clowns, the runaways, the juvenile delinquents or the withdrawn children who tried to "hide" in the classroom to escape their failures. This classification of students ultimately became known as the learning disabled. A person with a learning disability is a person who has an average or above average IQ but is not learning through the conventional methods of teaching. Learning-disabled children were typically described as those who didn't appear to be trying, and who "could, *if they would.*" But, in truth it's the reverse—they would, *if they could.* As their numbers began to increase dramatically, we could see that this particular type of child was showing measurable success in our program. This caused our school to become dually focused on children with functional disabilities and children with learning disabilities.

Rosemary Larson, co-founder and art therapist extraordinaire.

Several teachers and/or therapists had joined the effort by this time, and throughout the formative years Rosemary Larson was right there with me. Rosemary was an outstanding art therapy teacher. She could teach almost any subject through the medium of art in an amazingly interesting way. She was a master at working with the wide variety of children in our group; and, by applying different methods to each individual child's needs, we got some very good results. Of course, not everything we tried worked, but many things did! When something repeatedly failed, we would reassess, modify, change, or eliminate the method we were using. We did not accept failure until we had tried a particular tactic on a particular task numerous times. When it was time to give up on a certain approach, we had to find another way. We discovered that this trial and error and try again method was not only okay, but also a classic example of experiential learning. We're still doing it that way!

When something repeatedly failed, we would reassess, modify, change, or eliminate the method we were using.

JUMP-STARTING BRIARWOOD

With St. Philip's stipulation that we leave their buildings in three years, we knew that we would soon require a more permanent home. The Purdue methodology and good-old-common-sense approaches to curriculum were working very well, so we had a lot of children applying to be in the school. We knew that we could make our program even better in our own building, but that would take a good deal of money. Then, of course, we would need the proper design for a suitable building, a reputable and highly qualified contractor, and a good location—quite an undertaking!

God simply kept sending us what we needed to survive.

We believed that it *could* happen, but we had no idea whose door to knock on to raise the money.

Sally Woolrich, the wonderful principal of St. Francis Episcopal Day School who had encouraged me to talk to Memorial Drive Baptist Church earlier, now convinced me that the program we were giving birth to was a very important educational breakthrough—one that would not survive without a business plan. That plan, she said, would require charging tuition and raising money. Prior to St. Philip's we had done neither. How had this been possible? God simply kept sending us what we needed to survive, and He was always right on time.

Sheila Doran-Benyon, whom I mentioned previously, was one of those Godsends. God also sent us a physical therapist, an art therapist, a school administrator, a perceptual motor teacher, and other pertinent consultants who joined our motley crew—and not one of them was paid. They were true missionaries, each and every one.

During the same period of time, in what seemed like another part of my life, I received another nudge from a friend, Dossy Fondren Allday. Dossy and I were members of a highly unsuccessful investment club. After several years, we re-named it the "Buy High/Sell Low Investment Club," because that's all we seemed to be able to do; but we all enjoyed getting together. Dossy and I had visited about the work that was being done with these children with special needs and also about the stipulation that St. Philip's Church had given us. She appeared very interested.

A month or so later as I was doing my volunteer work at St. Francis, a lady from the office came down and said, "Yvonne, you're wanted on the phone." I went down to the office and answered the call. It was Dossy. She said that the Fondren Foundation wanted to give us $100,000 to get this program "on the ground." This was in the early 1970s—$100,000 is a tremendous amount today, but it was an unbelievable amount of money back then. That was a miracle and a catalyst especially since we hadn't formally asked for it! Dossy and I had just been talking, as friends do—and as a result of a conversation, a huge, unexpected

The Briarwood School circa 2009.

grant became the *starting point* for The Briarwood School and ultimately The Brookwood Community. That single, generous act changed our *destiny*. It allowed us to raise our sights from temporary buildings or borrowed Sunday School classrooms into a highly efficient and strategically-planned school facility. With this confidence-inspiring gift in hand, we went to other foundations and individuals to share

> That single, generous act changed our *destiny*.

our vision. We raised the money to buy ten acres of land and to design and build a 45,000-square-foot building for children with functional disabilities (the "Vickis" of this world) *and* for children with learning disabilities or differences. We began the design and build process in 1972; this school, now called Briarwood, has served more than 12,000 students since 1973 and has seen 87% of the learning disabled go on to college. That's quite an accomplishment for the students, and one for which the staff and the leadership of Briarwood really should be commended.

TEACHABLE MOMENTS

Every step of the process of learning to teach functionally-disabled and learning-disabled children has been full of challenges: ups and downs, building blocks of experience, brick walls, and smoothed-out paths. Each person comes with his or her unique gifts, challenges, and ways of learning, and many reward your diligent investment in their lives in unexpected ways.

> Each person comes with his or her unique gifts, challenges, and ways of learning.

One student, Tracy, was an example. I think his story is worth telling because it is representative of the confidence that we had to demonstrate to and for our students. Tracy was a young man who used daredevil tactics as an attention-getting device. He ran out in front of cars to scare the drivers. More than once, he climbed on the roof of the one-story church building when we were at Memorial Drive Baptist Church and refused to come down. We knew that he'd been kicked out of every school he had ever attended, a record he was quite aware of. He was very smart but completely uncooperative. One day when he was up on the roof, I went out to try and talk him down. I insisted he get off the roof *immediately;* and as I expected, he refused. Finally, after much conversation, he said, "Okay, I'll come down. But when I do, I am going to stab you in the laig." "Laig" is Texas-talk for leg. Well he did come down, and, as soon as he did, he picked up a good-sized stick and, as promised, stabbed me in the "laig." Not badly, but it happened. Then he lay down on the grass and refused to get up.

"Tracy," I said, in no uncertain terms, "I don't care *what* you do, you are not getting yourself kicked out of this school—and that's that."

He looked up at me and said, very plaintively, "But I stabbed you, Mrs. Streit."

"I know that," I told him, "and I don't care. I also know that you are a *very* smart boy who is confused about a lot of things right now. But that will *not* stop you from being a really good man and doing really good things, which I *know* you are capable of. So—*just do it.*"

> He had been rejected time and time again and we certainly didn't want to see that happen again.

Tracy looked at me for a few seconds without saying a word and then got up and went to class. He had been rejected time and time and we certainly didn't want to see that happen again. I know how that hurts because it had happened frequently to our daughter. I swore up and down I would never reject anybody just because in one way or another they were different, so I sure wasn't going to reject this boy. Later that day I went in to his class and said, "Tracy, you are a really great guy, and I like you." I asked him what he thought about our earlier conversation; he said (and I quote), "That was a bunch of B.S." That was not the response that I was hoping for.

"Well, okay," I said firmly, "but if you aren't 'chicken,' you might just try getting with it!" The school staff was trained to let him know repeatedly that they were "there for him" by their actions, words, and deeds—but the oppositional behavior continued for some time before it began to wane. Finally he *did* begin to make an effort to do his work and even surprised himself by his accomplishments. We were glad to see those changes, but we were also careful not to *ooooh* and *ahhhhh* too much over Tracy's progress. We just quietly and sincerely let him know that he was doing well. In this way, we were programming him for success, and each success gave him more confidence and then hope. This went on for months until he was able to go back to public school, where he did very well.

A few years ago, Tracy called me and said, "I want to come and see you. I want to see that school, because you all saved my life." When he came, he sat down in my office and surprised me by saying, "Mrs. Streit, I want to give a scholarship for a kid just like me." I jokingly said, "Thank you very much Tracy, but I don't think that there *is* another kid just like you. But we'll take the money anyway." And we both laughed. Sure enough, Tracy has grown up to be a good man who has accomplished a lot in his chosen field. You may know of him; his name is Woodrow Tracy Harrelson, and he's known in television and movies as Woody Harrelson.

Woody Harrelson revisits Briarwood with Joyce.

Construction of Briarwood.

LEARNING AND TEACHING

Throughout the nomadic journey from our backyard classroom to the Briarwood School, Vicki went with me, side-by-side all the way. She had been in every one of these facilities that we were in and even traipsed around with me as I went from door to door looking for that next place to go. She enjoyed her school time and, of course, the special "coaching" that she received at home during family time. Our whole family was involved in her therapy. I can't say that each one of us always enjoyed it, but it bonded us with a togetherness that has been a strong family asset. One of our girls told me once that it made her feel good that we all worked to help Vicki, because "if something happens to me, I know you'll take care of me, too!" She was right.

As a number of more severely involved children had joined us she had her own "set of friends," and these families learned to rely on each other. Even when we had no building and hardly any equipment, we did what we could with what we had. "Start where you are. Use what you have. Do what you can," said tennis-great Arthur Ashe. And we followed that advice.

As more and more students with learning disabilities came to us at Briarwood, Rosemary and I knew that the children with functional disabilities needed something different. If we could teach a learning-disabled child adequately, he or she would more than likely be equipped to go to college or find a job. However, the child with functional disabilities required more customized employment opportunities with proper supervision and support. Once again it was time to forge a new path.

We hired a young educator named Rick DeMunbrun from the State School in Austin to help us develop techniques to teach the students work skills—jobs that we would more than likely have to create and provide. We had to have additional revenue so we devised a plan: we would design and produce outstanding products and grow fabulous plants to help underwrite the needs of our community. We wanted to teach skills that would equip these individuals to contribute to the enterprises, and, in turn give them purpose, self-confidence, self-esteem, and a vital role in society.

> **We wanted to teach skills that would equip these individuals to contribute to the enterprises, and, in turn give them purpose, self-confidence, self-esteem, and a vital role in society.**

We began to ask ourselves and others who worked with the functionally disabled, "What do these individuals really need to give them the best life possible?" At the State School where Rick had worked in the early 1970s before coming to Briarwood, he had seen people who were cared for in a very paternalistic manner. Although their basic physical needs for food, clothing, and shelter were met, Rick felt that their very important emotional and social needs were not being met: they needed to know that they were valued and loved, and that they were *important*. Important is an *important* word at Brookwood.

We were seeing first hand that what functionally disabled adults needed wasn't a lot of academics, but projects that taught them how to actually do things and succeed. We combined the successes of skill development from Purdue with the needs that we saw in these folks and the outcome was self-esteem, enthusiasm, and turned-around, productive lives. Our vision for the next step on the educational journey became *real* work, rather than "pretend" work. The hard truth was that these individuals would never be whatever it is that we call "normal." Denial of that fact, by us or by their families, was becoming more harmful than helpful. They didn't need more "advanced levels" of education as much as they needed everyday life skills taught in tandem with their own potential. Quite simply put it is *practical education in tandem* with life. Although our teaching techniques had already taken us away from the educational path that was considered normal at the time, the time had come to take a radically different path. Through our experiences, we had come to firmly believe that with this new approach the functionally disabled could enjoy life "as-is," and others could enjoy it with them.

> **It is practical education in tandem with life.**

Many families of functionally-disabled students weren't ready to hear this, and plenty of educators were still trying to teach only the traditional curriculum. Our philosophy was to offer instruction in meaningful skills along with usable academics tailored for each individual's ability level. We were probably not the only people in the world that embraced this philosophy—but we were the only ones that we knew. Only a few voices were starting to suggest ideas that might work, and those voices were spread out around the world. Even so, we believed that hands-on productive skills would brighten the lives of our functionally-disabled students, because all people have the instinct to work, to produce, and to recognize their success. The challenge is to make the job fit the individual's passion and potential. The need to be needed is so important to all of us.

The need to be needed is so important to all of us.

Competitive employment had always tried to fit the functionally disabled, the "square pegs," into traditional "round hole" jobs. The idea for Brookwood began with the search for a practical solution in tandem with life: the creation of square-hole jobs so that "square pegs" could partially support themselves and prosper—socially, emotionally, and spiritually. Each new day brought new challenges as frequently as it brought the possibility of a breakthrough.

WE NEED SOMETHING DIFFERENT

The children with functional disabilities were definitely having success at the Briarwood School. Building self esteem works wonders plus the curricular emphasis on perceptual motor development, life skills, and productivity helped them become more physically and emotionally stable. It was a meaningful curriculum and served them well until they reached the age of twenty or twenty-one, when they would need to go someplace else and begin a different life. Then we were faced with the hard truth that there is generally no "graduation" from a functional disability. Specialized education is a lifelong need.

Building self esteem works wonders.

Yvonne and students at Briarwood.

There has been so much focus over the years—and rightly so—on helping children with disabilities, but we're only children for a quarter of our lives. We're adults for the other three-quarters! Very little attention was being given to the fact that we simply didn't know what to do with the adult with disabilities. Many of them couldn't truly succeed in a regular job, even one that they could do for a short period of time. Frequently, in normal employment they became anxious or began to act out, and these wonderful employers who were willing to hire them didn't know what to do. There were, of course, occasional success stories about a functionally-disabled man or woman who was able to keep a job for life; and that was wonderful, but, for the vast majority, this was not possible.

What were we going to do for Vicki, and for all of the others who were following our program? We needed something different for them. The recognition that there was no existing path for adults with functional disabilities was scary and discouraging, but it was also the very place where the journey to The Brookwood Community began in earnest.

We had no model to go by, so Rosemary and I started looking, quite literally, all over the United States and beyond—*again.* We went to Maryland, Florida, California, Pennsylvania, New York, Delaware, and all over Texas. We traveled to Europe as well.

In each place we visited, it seemed we found something positive. When we did, we'd tell ourselves, "You know, this idea would be really good for John, or Mike or Lynn." Another idea would be good for Joy, and still another for Bill, or Jack, or JoEllen. We could make these assessments because we really *knew* these children. Perhaps one of the most important results of all the dead ends I ran into through all of our experiences is that they allowed me to assimilate different ideas and methods and shape them into a program that could be individualized. Individualization was—and still is—very important to our work. Generally speaking, it is best to teach any student one-on-one. In this way the teacher can adapt (and keep on adapting) her tactics to that student's particular need. But the benefit of individualized instruction is far more important for the student with a functional disability. Instead of something merely desirable for learning, it becomes an almost essential element.

> **The benefit of individualized instruction is far more important for the student with a functional disability.**

One program we observed that stands out in my mind was the Lambs Farm in Libertyville, Illinois. This facility had a pet store, a bakery, and a tearoom. That tearoom was very appealing. I thought, "Gee, that would be great, but we're not ready for it yet. But let's catalog the idea and keep it for the future." I felt the pet store might be a viable option, too. But their bakery existed because the Sara Lee Corporation was just down the road from them and provided things for their residents to prepare and sell. We would have loved to collaborate with a great company like Sara Lee, but we decided that might be a longer commute than either of us wanted since they were just outside Chicago. One of the traps I have been a victim of on several occasions is the belief that if opportunity knocks I must immediately open the door and take that opportunity because it may not come by again. Of course, this is true to a point. But if you weaken your total program by adding more responsibility than you are able to properly handle at the time, you are not likely to advance your overall mission in a quality way. It is better to strengthen each aspect of your program and do it with excellence before venturing into unexplored waters, no matter how promising they may seem.

Another place we saw that was tremendously helpful to us was the Bethel Institution in Bielefeld, Germany. Today Bethel is one of Europe's largest Christian welfare services, with multi-faceted programs targeting many different disadvantaged populations. But their beginning was much simpler and quite stirring.

> **Strengthen each aspect of your program and do it with excellence before venturing into unexplored waters.**

The story we were told by our guide when we visited Bethel involved a German minister, Reverend Friedrich von Bodelschwingh, who had heard that epileptics were being taken out to the fields and left alone in huts because they were believed to be filled with evil spirits, a belief quite prevalent in the 1800s. The "powers that be" in the community did not intervene; and, of course, they couldn't make it on their own, and so they died. Reverend von Bodelschwingh was terribly offended by this, and one day he asked his congregation, "Are you aware that this is being done?"

The congregation confessed that they were, and von Bodelschwingh challenged them, "Don't you think we ought to do something about it?"

Of course they agreed. But then, like the rest of us, they walked out of church week after week, forgetting what they had purposed to do. Finally one day, von Bodelschwingh decided to take some of these abandoned epileptic citizens to church with him. He got them there early and had them sit in the front pews of the church, and then he started his sermon again about the shameful treatment of the epileptic. "Do you realize they're taking these folks out in the wild and leaving them to die?" he asked. Then again he challenged his parishioners, "Don't you think we ought to do something about it?"

As they had before, the parishioners agreed, "Oh, yes. We should." The reverend replied, pointing to the friends he had brought with him that day, "Well, good, because here are six we can start with." Some families took these folks in, and that worked so well that other epileptics came to the area, joined those six, and eventually a gigantic village known as Bethel ("house of God") grew up. Over the years, many Bethel folks were assimilated into the community and the villagers took care of them. Their charity and good works became known throughout the world. We visited Bethel and learned from them—especially in the area of providing work for the disabled. *I don't know if this story is exactly the way it happened but this is the way it was told to us when we were there and it touched us deeply.*

Considering all we had seen at Lambs Farm, Bethel, and many other places, we began to formulate a program at Briarwood that could provide meaningful work for the functionally disabled. We envisioned a program that would promote self-worth and allow our folks to create products that people would buy because they were *good*, not because they were made by people with special needs. One of our goals at Briarwood, and later at Brookwood, was to become largely self-sustaining. We do not take government money due to the additional staffing and administrative demands that accepting such funds would require, so we must have another way to support our programs.

We were not sure, at first, what the meaningful work that would be self-sustaining might be. Many of our initial attempts were spectacularly *unsuccessful*. The first year we worked with plants at Brookwood, we killed 97% of them—not a good survival rate! But even if the results were discouraging, we were learning a great deal. For example, to grow plants, we taught the students how to take the seedlings out of a seedling tray and place them in four-inch pots. Imagine trying to teach someone who doesn't understand the fragility of seedling plants how to be very gentle with them. It is quite a difficult undertaking; "gentle" is a challenging concept to teach! We had a lot of "green mush" from untrained hands that squeezed the plants too vigorously.

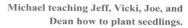

The first year we worked with plants at Brookwood, we killed 97% of them—not a good survival rate!

Michael teaching Jeff, Vicki, Joe, and
Dean how to plant seedlings.

Once again, we employed the hand-over-hand teaching technique I had been taught first by Dr. Kephart to use with Vicki. We would put our hands over theirs and push rather firmly, saying, "not gentle," or shaking our heads no if they were non-verbal. Then we would take our hand away. The next step was to touch their hands very softly and say, "gentle," and/or nod our heads yes. We'd do this again, and again, and again. Then we would ask them to do it to us so that we could be sure they understood.

Finally, our functionally disabled students were able to take the little baby plants out of the trays and put them very gently into the dirt. And sure enough, after a period of time—a rather long time—more and more plants survived, a horticulture operation was underway, and it became very successful. Today, many years and many mistakes later, Brookwood citizens propagate about 300,000 plants annually.

One day, not very long ago, we were taking a tour group through what has become a state-of-the-art horticulture enterprise at The Brookwood Community. As one of our citizens took small cuttings and planted them in four-inch pots, a visitor watching him said, "You know, I plant the plants you grow here and they live and are beautiful, but I've never had a green thumb before. Usually nothing I plant ever blooms." This citizen very matter-of-factly turned to the woman and said, "That's because God holds my hand while I work on the plants." The visitor was visibly moved, and after a few moments she said, "Well then, thanks to both of you."

Making ceramics is another big endeavor at Brookwood today, and it, too, first began as an "experiment" at Briarwood. Our ceramics products were really so bad in the beginning that we jokingly said, "Even the garbage men don't want to pick up our stuff." We were making ceramic leaves and other ornamental designs that no one recognized, and I think we sold about six of these to sympathetic parents. Then some brilliant team member said, "Why not try cookie cutter Christmas ornaments?" So we did. Those ornaments were a success and have become one of our mainstay products in ceramics. Since that initial process of trial and error, Brookwood has

> In our efforts to prove that we could teach the "unteachable," we tried many and varied ideas.

made and sold some 100,000 Christmas ornaments to delighted customers over the years.

In our efforts to prove that we could teach the "unteachable," we tried many and varied ideas. One was woodworking. With a very well-protected blade for safety, we began making little puzzle manger scenes and then three-legged stools. After we got well into the project, we realized that cutting the wood precisely was not all that doable for our students or staff for that matter—so we moved on.

We tried shell-covered nightlights; but these did not give us enough return for the time spent, and the market for them was limited. We made candle-holders out of large red and/or green ashtrays that were fairly popular at first, but the non-smoking era was moving in and ash trays were moving out, so that endeavor didn't last long.

We also tried our hand at enterprises that had traditionally been assigned to the handicapped, like caning chair seats, cutting stakes for Houston Lighting and Power and, of all things, sorting wire coat hangers. The sorting of the coat hangers nearly drove us all nuts. Those tangled, jumbled up, Rubik's® cubes of wire seemed to me like punishment that would test the likes of Job. It was a horrendous task! Cutting stakes was not much better; demand for them was limited and the cost of doing the job far outweighed the benefits of accomplishment and contribution that our citizens received for their effort.

As challenging as these tasks were, it was the caning of chairs that really taught us that these traditional enterprises for the disabled were not the answer for us. Caning chairs is a very difficult thing to do properly. With the amount of supervision required, *and* the learning curve, *and* the wasted supplies, we found the cost of a single seat to be about

Risk-taking is common when previously standard practices are being challenged.

$800! That added to the cost of the chair itself meant that we didn't have too many takers.

Our experiments with enterprises proved that we would need to come up with our own ideas and our own processes in order to make good, saleable products. Perhaps just as important, we realized that we needed to have another setting in which to produce items and operate these enterprises with our students. Once again we faced the old risk, with which we were becoming well acquainted. But then, risk-taking is common when previously standard practices are being challenged.

WHERE CAN WE GO?

Our vision for the long-term flourishing of the many "Vickis" at Briarwood was coming into focus. We dreamed of a place where our folks could be accepted as they were, where they didn't need to be "fixed," and where they could feel safe and loved. We also dreamed of a place where they could be taught skills that would make them feel good about themselves and where they could function and see themselves as important contributing members of society. We believed we

> We dreamed of a place where our folks could be accepted as they were, where they didn't need to be "fixed."

were developing a program that would work, but we needed to effectively house that program. Where could we go to put that dream into action? We wanted an ample piece of land that was near a metropolitan area but not in it, near a freeway but not on it, and pretty, because we wanted the best for our students, who would ultimately call themselves citizens of this new community.

The next step was to introduce our very unconventional dream of a "country place" to some highly-regarded and visionary Houstonians who might open doors for us, people who were able to envision our concept for living and learning and who could think outside the box. It was up to us to help them understand how different our strategy was from the conventional methods of the day, and to realize its potential impact on this ever-increasing population. We needed them to help us make it happen.

I knew in my heart that this concept would work, but how was I supposed to convince people who hardly knew a person with disabilities, much less have one that they cared deeply about? How could we convey to them our passion to go after this goal? I made an appointment with Randy Smith and Jack Trotter, two very powerful and influential leaders in the city and state, who also happened to be two of my long-time friends.

Randy and I were baptized at the same time as babies at the First Methodist Church in downtown Houston by his father, Bishop A. Frank Smith, so we really had known each other for a long time. He became a highly respected lawyer and a partner in Vinson & Elkins, a worldwide law firm headquartered in Houston. Randy was an outstanding community servant; a national lay leader in the United Methodist Church; a godly, fine, smart, hardheaded man; and a good friend. He ultimately enlisted the support of this law firm, *which has played a vital role in the development and sustaining of Brookwood.*

I had known Jack since our high school days. He was a few years ahead of me, and even in those days he was king of the hill—just a superstar and very, very smart. This financial genius served on the Board of Directors at Rice University, where notable people from far and wide sought his counsel. He was always there for me when I needed someone to join me in thinking "outside the box."

I thought, "You know, if I could convince Randy and Jack about our plan, and if they agreed to help, we could probably make it happen." So I made an appointment with the two of them, drove downtown from the Briarwood School, and quite literally, prayed all the way. I went into Jack's office and told these two good men about our dream, described the need, and explained how we believed it could be accomplished. When I finished talking, there was dead silence in the room—something very unusual for either of them.

Finally, Randy looked me straight in the eye and asked, "Yvonne, do you think that this is the will of God?"

I immediately answered with a strong, "Yes! Yes I do."

Silence fell again for what seemed like a long time, but was probably only a few seconds.

Then Jack said, "If we do this, we'll have to put something on the ground, because most people will not understand it unless they experience it—and they certainly won't envision the potential unless they actually *see* it working. Now Yvonne, that will mean borrowing money, and I know how you feel about *that*. But we are going to have to do it if we're going to make people understand."

I nodded in agreement. Again, there was silence. Then both men said with strong conviction, "Let's do it. Let's get started."

I cannot tell you how unbelievably grateful I was. I felt strongly that I had already gotten a green light from God—and now the idea would have the support of two very encouraging and resourceful people here on earth.

> **"Let's do it. Let's get started."**

With this commitment made, we began trying to raise money, and we got exactly nowhere. I talked to many, many Rotary, Exchange, and Kiwanis Clubs in the city of Houston and its surrounding areas, and to any church that would let me in the door. This went on for two years. All the while I was still at Briarwood, trying to make sure that it was running properly, and that the teaching techniques we'd worked so hard to develop were being embedded into our school's culture through consistent practice. A lot of my focus was still on Briarwood, but because of the vacuum that existed for the adult with special needs, the Brookwood dream kept rushing in on me like a tsunami.

After two unsuccessful years of pounding the pavement, I began to think that perhaps this wasn't the will of God, after all. Maybe I had somehow missed His message, and I needed to stop this "pie in the sky" dream. This excruciating thought occurred to me on a Tuesday; we were to have a Board meeting on Thursday. It seemed to me that the only right thing to do was to tell them how I was feeling and then possibly throw in the towel. Within an hour or so, after that tremendously heartrending decision, the phone rang. It was Frank, a man from one of the Rotary Clubs where I had spoken.

"Yvonne," he said, "I'd like to stop by and bring you something tomorrow if that's okay. I could come by in the morning on my way to work."

"Well, that'd be great" I told him. "Just come on by."

So at about 8:00 the next morning, Wednesday, Frank arrived. We visited for a few minutes, but I still wasn't sure why he had come. Then he said, "I want to give you this check for you to study the Country Place." That was the name we were calling Brookwood at that time. The check was for $10,000. I nearly fainted. I couldn't believe it—after all of this time of pounding on doors! I saw him out the front door, turned around, and was met by my assistant principal, who was coming down the hall, saying, "Yvonne, you're not going to believe this, but Chester from that Rotary Club just called and wants to give us $7,500 to study the Country Place." My golly, we danced and jumped up and down, and thought, "My gosh, isn't that amazing? Isn't that something?"

At 9:30 a.m., while we were still doing happy gymnastics, the phone rang again. It was a representative of St. Luke's United Methodist Church who said, "Yvonne, we want to give you $25,000 to study the Country Place." We stopped our dancing and our carrying on long enough to realize that God was letting us know, through the affirming actions of others, that it was indeed His will for Brookwood to be born. His message was clear: "*This is a go.*" We had not misinterpreted His will, and He wanted to be sure we knew it.

God was letting us know, through the affirming actions of others, that it was indeed His will for Brookwood to be born.

But that's not the end of the story. That very same day at 11:00 a.m., the Barrow Foundation called, pledging to give us $30,000 to "study the Country Place." To this day, as I re-tell the story, I experience goose bumps and the realization that God is indeed present and will lead us in His way as we work and pray. God was speaking to us, not in words, but through these actions and through a spiritual sense that is truly *beyond all human understanding*, and He had given us a green light. So, the journey to Brookwood began with God's strong guidance and the generosity of others.

FINDING OUR FOREVER HOME

I'm not sure how many miles I put on my car within these two years looking for land within a 70-mile radius of the city of Houston; my secretary believed it was about 4,000 miles. All of this was going on after my work at Briarwood was done for the day. Thank goodness for the summer months and those extra hours of daylight, so that I could get out and around for a longer period of time.

After several months of hunting on our own, we realized we were going to have to pay a realtor to help us find some land. Rosemary and I located a really good agent in Fulshear, Texas, who knew the area quite well, and could steer us clear of the flood plain and help us find something well suited to our needs. That man worked in a ramshackle old building in Fulshear, but he was a true delight. He knew everybody in his "neck of the woods," as he said, and he soon began talking to Rosemary and me about "one piece of land that I really think might be the answer to your needs." He suggested we go there first, and so off we went.

He drove us about a mile south of Brookshire, where he showed us 475 acres of beautiful land. "We don't need that much land," I protested, but he said, "Well, let's just look at it. Let's just look and see."

Sure enough, it was so pretty. The western boundary was Bessie Creek, a picturesque little tributary of the mighty Brazos River. The north side overlooked a beautiful ranch owned by Betty and Cletus Brown, who would become some of our dearest friends and helpers. To the east about eight miles down the road was Katy, Texas, a growing suburban community, and on the south was some beautiful rolling land used for grazing cattle. It *was* a great place, but it was big—and the price was much too high.

Even so, as we stood and looked at it, I said to myself, "This is it." I didn't realize I'd spoken audibly, but Rosemary was standing next to me and she said, "No, Yvonne, you didn't just think it. I heard you say: *'This is it.'*" What a wonderful feeling to get a clear answer after working diligently for something for such a long time!

It was another green light for us. We had gathered our forces and begun, and we had been lead to the perfect piece of land, but our next step was an enormous challenge. We were entering the 1980s, and the oil business showed signs of difficulty. Houston money—foundations and individuals—is and has long been tremendously dependent on the oil industry. So with that oil bubble bursting, it became a double whammy. We took the facts, the figures, and our concept back to the Board who then studied the idea and the land—and with courage and faith agreed that we should move ahead. For the first time in the history of Briarwood we decided to break our rule about borrowing money. We just had to do it to buy the land we needed to put our dream on the ground. With land and a plan we could let people see this revolutionary program in action. We borrowed the money, and bought the land on the last day of December, New Year's Eve, 1981.

The property had once been part of an original grant to the Republic of Texas statesman Stephen F. Austin, now known as The Father of Texas. We still have a copy of the original deed with his signature on it. An old farmhouse stood on this land, built, we were told, in 1932. In realtor-speak it was "quaint," which meant the foundation had cracked and the roof was bad. There was also a garage, an outdoor cookhouse, and a few rundown chicken coops. That was it as far as improvements.

> "People helping people" was a cornerstone of Brookwood in those early years, and it still is today.

We decided that we could use the farmhouse, because the damaged roof didn't actually leak, although why it didn't, I don't know. And, there was one bathroom.

Our first project out on the Country Place was to plant some pine trees. We had heard that the State was giving away pine seedlings to anyone who would plant them. We obtained about 2,000 of these little seedlings, and got the Key Club seniors at Briarwood to plant them for us as a service project. Once the group decided to take on the project, we hosted a big day where twenty-five or so teachers and students planted 2,000 pine trees; but it didn't rain, and we didn't water. As a result, every one of those 2,000 trees died. That was our first big, "fall-on-your-face" mistake at Brookwood—although many others would follow.

We may have failed the first time, but we did not give up. Free trees were still available, so we got another 2,000 and tried again. This time we did a little bit of watering, and more of those trees lived. In fact, quite a few of them are still growing on our campus today. Every time I look at them, I think of those Briarwood seniors and the teachers who came out and planted them for us—twice. "People helping people" was a cornerstone of Brookwood in those early years, and it still is today.

When we began operating at Brookwood in 1983, we offered a day program for the functionally disabled, taking those students from Briarwood out to Brookwood in a bus we bought with funds from a caring sorority. They gave us the money and we found a bus. It was a very handsome bus but not quite as mechanically sound as it might have been. Yes, we "kind-of" had it checked out, but in spite of the mechanic's once-over it tended to sputter and cough periodically and then just stop. He kindly suggested that we bring it by at least once a week so that he could check it and make sure it was working properly. If we didn't want to do that (since the problem wasn't *too* serious), then all we had to do to keep it running was to pull off the highway, twist some gizmo under the hood, and then pound on the carburetor while singing the Star Spangled Banner backwards.

A Briarwood teacher and one of the students planting the infamous pine trees at Brookwood.

After that, we would be ready to go! I *am* kidding about the Star Spangled Banner part, but his do-it-yourself instruction seemed about as impractical as all that to us. So we went another way. We knew that we needed a bus driver, so our solution was to hire a bus driver who was also a mechanic. Abraham was our second hire for Brookwood and he is with us today. He kept that bus running, and he and that bus have served us well.

Early on at Brookwood it was very difficult to get staff. The experienced teachers who we found wanted a regular classroom, one with books and desks and a chalkboard. Try as we might, we could not convince some of them that learning could take place while doing—in other words, practical education in tandem with life. They could not yet understand that active, experiential learning and avoiding failure if at all possible, would work.

> **God's green light for us to "Go" did not mean that we would not encounter any more challenges.**

So we started with untrained staff, and the teaching took place in the work areas, which served as classrooms. After all, God's green light for us to "*Go*" did not mean that we would not encounter any more challenges. It *did* mean that He would be with us, and if we worked together in good faith, it would happen.

Our day program at Brookwood began in the farmhouse, as well as a portable building that St. Luke's United Methodist Church gave us, and in four greenhouses given to us by River Oaks Garden Club and The Garden Club of Houston. (The portable building and all four of the greenhouses are still in use today, thirty-three years later.) During this start up time we really kept God busy rescuing us. As I look back I am truly amazed and ever so thankful that He was there to catch us time after time. So, blessed once again by the generosity of others, we began woodworking and created a classroom devoted to developing skills in our students for the cultivation of plants and the production of handcrafted products.

> *Everything* that you see today at The Brookwood Community began in the old farmhouse: our ceramics, stone casting, screen printing, clinic, dining room, offices, and even a simulated greenhouse.

The old farmhouse, as I said, was vintage 1932. It contained a living room and dining room, a kitchen, one useable bathroom, and three bedrooms. We took it over, using every available inch of space. Almost

The farmhouse, Brookwood's first building.

everything that you see today at The Brookwood Community began in the old farmhouse: our ceramics, stone casting, screen printing, clinic, dining room, offices, and even a simulated greenhouse. To say we were crowded was an understatement. There was a potential classroom upstairs in the re-finished attic, but the floor was so weak it wobbled and bowed. But because we needed the space, we had a support for the floor built by a neighboring builder who volunteered for us on the weekends. He took a look and said it could be fixed but in a rather unconventional way. He and his crew put a huge metal disc under the attic floor for support, then connected it with a big chain to the rafters at the peak of the roof, stabilizing the floor. Of course that, in turn, "decorated" the ceiling of the living room downstairs in a rather unique way, but our attic space was secure.

Once this was done we had a nice, safe classroom for teaching our citizens various skills to use in their handcrafting enterprises.

In the beginning thirty or so people worked in or around that farmhouse with only one working bathroom, so we learned to schedule more efficiently than you can possibly imagine. One bathroom isn't really the answer to thirty people's needs, but I can tell you this: it was the cleanest bathroom you have ever seen.

It was just amazing to hear the comments from visitors after they came out to that beat-up old farmhouse, the donated greenhouses, and the garage where we had begun doing stone casting. One said, "You know, this is not at all what I expected. I came here with my friend thinking, 'I don't really want to go,' but much to my surprise I'm leaving with a smile on my face, and the sense that something wonderful is happening out there. These folks are so happy that it makes *me* happy." Others would tell us, "You know, y'all need a store to sell some of these products," and, "I think that you could turn this living room into a store." They really thought that at least *some* of our products would sell, and of course that thrilled the staff and all of the citizens. Still, we had a long way to go before we could produce the quality of craftsmanship that we have reached today.

So we cleaned out the living room and set up our first small store. We hadn't made very many things at the time, but we had some Christmas ornaments, a couple of ceramic bowls, and a Santa Claus from stone casting. Hayden Larson, Rosemary's oldest son, designed some really great things for stone casting. There was a sun face with all of the rays coming out from it, and a series of plaques representing summer, winter, fall and spring. They were beautiful, and our citizens had learned to finish them really well. We were not doing any tea-staining or highlighting then, just offering the product as it came out of the mold, polished up with soft gloves and some fine steel wool. Later on the use of tea stain and burnt umber made these products come alive.

Some of our volunteers made products for that first store, too, such as some place mats hand-painted with Texas wildflowers. Parents and friends brought us things that they made, and when we had a sale, there were always plenty of homemade cookies on hand. These small and simple events were wonderful and a great motivator for us all. Our citizens were learning how to do handwork, and they were so proud of each and every piece. We only had a few customers—mostly the parents and families of our students, because at that point in time no one else was eager to buy what we were able to make. But we were learning!

While we weren't yet proficient in making or growing things, something far more important was being "built" in that farmhouse. We began to hear more comments like, "This place just makes me feel good," or "I can't get over how happy all of these people seem to be, and that includes the staff. It's something I can't put my finger on. There is a *spirit* in this place." A visitor made this comment to one of our citizens and she told him that that was because, "God is teaching my teacher how to teach me, and I like that." We realized there was a presence at Brookwood, and it's still here. We know that if you take time to look behind the scenes you will see a lot of so-called coincidences—but we know that coincidences are God's little miracles in disguise.

> While we weren't yet proficient in making or growing things, something far more important was being "built" in that farmhouse.

EVEN THE BEST PATHS HAVE PUDDLES

We had come a long way from those first dark days when Vicki began having seizures. Slowly we had begun to learn that there was a plan, and although it didn't always make sense to us, if we let God be in control, amazing things would happen. We had come to understand that we were working not only to help our daughter and her friends, but all the functionally disabled. The Brookwood story that began in our backyard in the 1960s, then took root in a series of temporary, well-intended but short-lived "homes" throughout the city, began to emerge as a green sprout at the Briarwood School and to grow in earnest in a farmhouse in Brookshire, Texas.

That old building housed a dedicated staff (the most important ingredient to any program), who sometimes had to make or bring their own equipment, picked up spare paperclips found on sidewalks to bring to work, and brought pencils and paper from home. We had no typewriter at first, and wrote all our letters and instructions by hand. And there was *very* little money.

What *did* we have? We had purpose, and anyone with eyes to see and ears to hear could recognize the hand of God at work as Brookwood grew under His leadership. Folks with special needs were not dismissed as useless, but were viewed as wonderful human beings on a different path—one with a lot of puddles! Our teachers wanted others to know that these students were great and productive individuals having a different adventure on this journey called life. We are all spiritual beings having a human experience.

As we made the move to Brookwood, a powerful transition was taking place: a transition from "I am your caretaker" to one of "Let's become partners on an interdependent path to purpose." I cannot point to a certain part in the story or a certain time on the calendar that this transition began. It emerged as we followed a series of nudges from God and learned from our experiences with our "true teachers"—the Brookwood citizens themselves. I heard often in those early days how lucky we were to have so many wonderful things happening for us. I guess lucky could be the word, but this comment always reminded me of a saying I once heard, "I find that the harder I work under God, the luckier I get."

> A powerful transition was taking place: a transition from "I am your caretaker" to one of "Let's become partners on an interdependent path to purpose."

What we had begun teaching the functionally disabled when we were still at Briarwood to prove to ourselves that it *could* be done was now taking place in a different setting. This success led us to understand even more about our unique students. They had experienced so much failure in their lives that they really didn't want to try anything new only to fail again. Therefore we began to continually ask ourselves and each other:

- How can we present a project so that our students will feel good about doing the task?
- Through which sensory inputs—visual, auditory, tactile, kinesthetic or motor—does each student receive information most readily?
- In what setting does each student most readily receive the information?
- Can we conduct the teaching in an actual work environment that is unlike a classroom?
- Can we teach/instill in them the satisfaction that comes from the meaningful end results of their work?
- Can we create situations where the proper response is demanded—where the *situation* becomes the motivator rather than the *instructor*?

We had proved that through creativity and perseverance, the majority of those previously considered unteachable are truly teachable.

HOW DO WE SUSTAIN THIS?

We still did not want to apply for government funding. It would come with too many restrictions, and we felt that with time and proper teaching, we could use the old American free enterprise system and "make it on our own." We anticipated three sources of revenue working in tandem for us: donations, tuition, and proceeds from our citizen enterprises.

In the beginning, donations represented by far the largest percentage of our funding. Tuition was also contributing revenue, but many families couldn't afford the full amount of our tuition cost, so we gave them financial aid. Over the years, the amount of that tuition aid has grown, and currently we provide approximately one million dollars per year for that purpose. Our third source of income is our enterprise division that began with those three-legged little stools and nightlights and now consists of original handcraft products, consumables, and horticulture. We strive to produce saleable products in order to help subsidize the community. In the beginning, however, not only were these enterprises not making money, they were costing us money. We were facing an uphill battle and we knew we had to try another way.

In addition to the challenges we faced in figuring out how to make the enterprises something that could provide on-going valuable work for the citizens, as well as revenue for the community, we once again ran into people who did not understand what we were doing. While most folks got it the minute they saw the Brookwoodians engaged in their work, some questioned the benefit to our citizens. One day I was leading a group of educators on a tour of Brookwood. After an introductory explanation of what we try to do here, one man, who seemed to have a rather large chip on his shoulder, said, "The way you are making those people work seems like slave labor."

"We don't feel that way," I told him, "and we know that our citizens don't. They want to contribute and feel needed. The need to be needed is so important to all of us." Then I told him and the rest of the tour group about Bill, who at one time was our star basketball player.

When Bill first came to Brookwood all he wanted to do was play basketball. We didn't have a regular gym in any sense of the word, just a gravel driveway and a goal and backstop that resembled the Leaning Tower of Pisa. We typically played there, but as a special treat we went into Briarwood once a week to play in their gymnasium—and that was a big deal. A few months after his arrival, Bill came to me and said he wanted to ask me a question.

"Great," I said, "go for it."

"I want to know if I have to go into Briarwood to practice basketball," he said. I was shocked to hear him say this, because I thought he loved basketball.

"No," I told him, "you don't have to go if you don't want to."

"Whew!" Bill said with visible relief. "You see, now I have a job, and I'm important."

Work is a vital part of our citizens' lives— just as it is for us.

After several similar incidents, we became convinced that work is a vital part of our citizens' lives—just as it is for us. After the tour, the same man approached me privately and said, "I certainly understand why Bill said what he did. These people *are* proud of themselves, and it gives me a good feeling and a new perspective. Thank you."

Another incident underscoring these feelings about work occurred in the ceramics studio. I happened to be sitting at a table with several of the students when one of them said to me, "Mrs. Streit, why do you call us students? I don't like that word, because it sounds like we are still in school. I don't like school. I have a *real* job and I'm good at it." Another student chimed in and agreed, so we all decided right then and there that we needed another name for ourselves. Believe it or not, we quickly and unanimously agreed on *citizen*. We then discussed this with another knowledgeable group and talked about prestige, maturity, willingness to care for others, and personal responsibility. Everyone agreed that they would try to live up to those common goals. We haven't always been able to do that, (I guess that is true everywhere), but we make an effort—and that counts, because we find that effort can become a positive action, positive actions become habits, and habits can shape a life.

TAKING THE SHOW ON THE ROAD

As our day students were working in the new greenhouses and in the old farmhouse, our dream was materializing. The plants our citizens planted were actually growing but we needed access to larger numbers of plant stock. I asked my church friends if they could think of a way we could get some cuttings, grow some plants in about six months, and then possibly have a little bazaar.

Together we came up with the idea of taking cuttings of Asiatic jasmine from our yards and bringing them back to the church. There, we would trim them and package them to take out to Brookwood. Asiatic jasmine is a tough plant, and our citizens needed tough plants to work with at this stage of their development.

We did this, and after counting the cuttings, we decided that we didn't have enough; so back out to the neighborhood we went. If we saw Asiatic jasmine growing in someone's yard, we went up to the door, rang the bell, told them about our project, and asked if we could take some cuttings. We were warmly welcomed by all, and we obtained an ample supply.

We then took the cuttings out to Brookwood where our citizens planted them in four-inch pots under the supervision of their teachers. Citizens dipped each cutting in root stimulator, planted it in pots that had been filled with soil by other citizens, and then took the little plants to their growing places. Five months later, after much TLC, we took them to our first Westminster United Methodist Church bazaar and sold them *back* to the wonderful ladies and their neighbors and friends who had provided us with them in the first place. What great people! We made a grand total of $183 at that bazaar, and we felt like we were on our way.

Vita teaching Laura.

Encouraged by this taste of success we decided to hold more bazaars. We began to have them at homes or churches, and even at some businesses. One of the successful ones we've done over the years has been a realty company bazaar held at their offices before Mother's Day. Later we tried our hand at the "big-time" Nutcracker Market, a giant holiday extravaganza benefiting the Houston Ballet. We have enjoyed success at that bazaar and at several others, but we quickly learned how challenging bazaars can be.

One year, we were involved in no less than twenty-three bazaars, a feat that represented more work than you can imagine. Not only did we have to design and create the products, we also had to go into inventory, pick out the items we wanted to take to each bazaar, wrap them up, pack them into trucks, take them to the church or organization, unload them, unwrap them, and display them on our hand-made tables. Then, those items that didn't sell had to be re-wrapped, packed, and returned to Brookwood, unloaded, unwrapped, and put back into inventory again. This was very time consuming, labor intensive, and exhausting—but the silver lining of our experience with the bazaars was that it told us, in no uncertain terms, that if we really wanted to sell products then we needed to have a store.

And there were other silver linings as well: The volunteers who manned those bazaars were absolutely wonderful. The bazaars themselves made Brookwood more visible, and they allowed others to learn more about our mission and to discover that at least some of the products we made were of high quality. Despite these wonderful benefits, we needed a more efficient sales venue: another nudge, another step forward, another building block, another wonderful challenge.

BUILDING A COMMUNITY

As our citizens became more and more successful and as philanthropic groups showed their willingness to support this rather revolutionary Brookwood community, we realized the time had come for our students to *live* at Brookwood. In residence, they could be provided the optimum environment for their success. Our trained staff could determine the citizens' asset avenues of learning, teach social skills, assign and teach home chores, and demonstrate ways to help each other. We knew that every opportunity to find success in even the smallest task could become a major step in skill and emotional development for them.

> Every opportunity to find success in even the smallest task could become a major step in skill and emotional development.

In 1984, Sasaki, Walker and Associates (SWA) did a pro bono master plan for The Brookwood Community and we have followed that master plan to this day. They did a fantastic job for us, and with a plan in place we began building: three resident homes and the Inn, which houses thirty-three citizens, the administrative offices, a dining room, and a health clinic, completed in 1985. Greg Glauser and his wife Andrea were the first home teachers at the Inn, and Greg still serves as our Spiritual and Citizen Life Director, our very own Pied Piper of Hamelin. One of the houses we constructed was for Rick DeMunbrun and his family. Magda, Rick's wife, was our nurse; and at the time, their family included three girls, Nicole, Courtney, and Laura, with baby Cynthia on the way. The second house was for our residential coordinator, and the third house was an intake house, which we used to introduce new citizens to Brookwood and get them acclimated to their surroundings. This house was under the direction of a very capable teacher who was an exceptional educational "detective." He could learn more about a person by observation in a few weeks than most people could learn in a year. We don't use that intake procedure anymore, because, as so often happens here, we found a better way. We now observe potential citizens through a series of "day visits" prior to their becoming a resident.

The Inn and Wellness Center.

The initial requests for residential placement were great. As soon as we opened our doors and said that we would offer a residential option, we were full. Or we *would* have been full, had we been able to take students as quickly as they applied. We had a critically important, lengthy procedure for really getting to know each candidate prior to admission. I am not referring to a traditional system, but to the far more important process of establishing trust. Trust is the bedrock, the cornerstone of a relationship. We knew we had to *earn* trust, and that takes time.

A couple of rooms in the Inn were initially designated for parents or visitors who might wish to come and stay with us for a few days. At that time, there was no place to stay nearby, and "Houston proper" was nearly twenty-five miles away. One couple, Bette and Bill Roberts, had enrolled their son Chad in the new residential program. They were moving to London, and they wanted us to have these rooms available when they came back to see Chad. He moved in before we really had the program up and running, but he was happy as a "bug in a rug," and still is today. Those designated guest rooms never got to be used as we intended. They quickly became needed for new citizens with whom we had previously established that critical component—trust.

DEDICATION

Our formal dedication of Brookwood took place in November of 1985. At least a couple hundred people attended the event that day. It was a very nice ceremony, and we were quite fortunate to have Barbara Bush as our very special guest speaker. We were all awed by her. In addition to Mrs. Bush's meaningful remarks, I do remember one incidental thing—the weather. We had experienced a series of very rainy days prior to the event—Houston-type downpours—and of course, we were planning to have the dedication outside, because we didn't have room inside for the numbers we were expecting. Marion and C. Fred Chambers, the parents of our citizen Margaret Chambers, suggested that we ask Barbara Bush to come. They offered to invite her, because they had been very close friends of the Bushes for years. They asked and, sure enough, got a positive response. We were ecstatic.

Barbara Bush gave an inspiring talk, and, as usual, captivated the audience and everyone with whom she spoke that day. Mrs. Bush is one of the most outstanding human beings you would ever want to meet. She's very straightforward, but diplomatic; both perceptive and receptive; a good listener; very smart; and has a terrific sense of humor. We were counting on this last asset, since on the day she was coming we were considering asking how we could get Noah to lend us his ark! A tsunami of rain hit that day.

The gathering clouds and rain early in the day threatened our plan to even have a dedication outside, and it was far too late to get a tent. This was certainly not an earth-shattering, global threat, but it was big to us in Brookshire, Texas, on that historic day. Believe it or not the rain stopped about 1:00 p.m., three hours before the ceremony was scheduled to begin, and it didn't rain again until about 6:00 p.m. when everyone was leaving. It seems insignificant now, but it felt like another miracle for us at the time.

Dedication ceremony with Barbara Bush.

Although the buildings had just been dedicated, the demand for residential space continued, and soon we were out of room. People were ready to move in, and we didn't have a place for them. We addressed this need by adding two new group homes, the Anderson and the Meadows. The Anderson home accommodated ten ladies, and the Meadows had space for ten men. Both filled up rather rapidly, and, in the meantime, we added four more greenhouses. Our program was expanding, but we were still conducting our classroom/workshops, as we called them at that time, in the old farmhouse. We call the workshops studios now, because the citizens who work there are truly artisans. To accommodate their work, we added the crafts building in 1988. It contains studios for ceramics and stone-casting, as well as a design and mold-making center.

Buildings are important, of course, and we are thankful for our beautiful campus today. But the heart and soul of Brookwood is what goes on beyond its doors, with the people our buildings exist to serve. The wonderful spirit we feel here, and visitors often note, was evident even when we were in the old farmhouse and the portable buildings. That spirit reflects the sincere realization of God's presence with us at all times. Even though sometimes we forget to acknowledge it, it's critically important to remember that it is His presence that allows us to say—Brookwood—where the spirit soars. And that's one of our mottoes: "Brookwood—where the spirit soars."

> It is His presence that allows us to say—
> "Brookwood—where the spirit soars."

GOD IS PRESENT WHETHER BIDDEN OR UNBIDDEN

One hallmark of The Brookwood Community since our earliest days has been our willingness to let the community evolve. We needed to seek ways to identify the needs of each individual, the needs of the community as a whole, and the requirements of each situation. And, we were and are open to the opportunities that come our way—even the ones that take us by surprise. One day, for example, the brother of one of our citizens sent me an article from the *Dallas Morning News* about a new foundation that was being formed. When I read it and saw that their goals were aligned to the goals of Brookwood, I thought that we might be a good fit. I wrote to them and described what we were doing; they responded that they would like to come down to see us and investigate. They did just that. During a question-and-answer time following their tour, they asked, "What is it that you most need?"

"Well, it's very difficult," I told them, "because we need so many things. But I think one of the most important things is a larger lunch room. Our folks eat rather slowly, and our lunchroom is so small we can only serve half of the citizens at one time, so some have to start eating around 10:30 a.m., and they don't finish until about noon. Then, by the time we get them out and the next group in, some are still eating at 2 p.m. That takes up a humongous part of the day. So we really do need a lunchroom."

Mealtime scheduling was indeed a big challenge, but so was administrative workspace. So I went on: "And then we also need some administrative space. Some of our staff have their office in a closet—and even though we painted a window on the wall, they say they still feel a little cramped." In fact, one of our administrators carried a cardboard box around with her because she didn't have a desk *or* a closet.

"We also need a visitors' center," I told our guests. "We have so many visitors, and they have no place to congregate or even sit down, so we need a place to host them. *And*, we need a gym; we desperately need a gym! Fitness is critical to our citizens' wellbeing, and right now we only have a gravel driveway and a lop-sided backboard for our basketball court." At this point, they were still listening intently, so I took a deep breath and kept going. "Then there's water therapy," I said. "We think aqua therapy is so important, and requires a pool, and we need a place for the pool, and we'd like for it to be indoors so we could use it year-round."

They looked at us, nodding, but they said, "Well, that's all well and good, but we can only give you one building."

So being creative thinkers, we designed one long, sectional building that held the visitors' center first, then the administrative wing, the lunchroom, the gymnasium, and a water park-type pool. It's all under one roof, we reasoned; consequently it's just one building. Apparently they agreed, because they gave us $5.5 million for that building, with the stipulation that we raise 1/5 of the total—$1.1 million—as an endowment. And, they asked that we display a bust of their founder in the Visitors Center, which we were quite happy to do! They wanted the Visitors' Center to be a very special, elegant space—and we did too, because we welcome over 50,000 guests each year! They told us that once we secured a commitment for the endowment they would execute the grant. Our response was *Hallelujah!*

So with the promise of our first major building grant before us, it was up to us to secure the $1.1 million required for the endowment. After the foundation's visit, I reported their gift to our Advisory Board. This group included Randy Smith, the partner at Vinson & Elkins LLP who was my right arm and one of God's great ambassadors; Jim Lesch, who was head of Hughes Tool Company; Brian O'Brien, the head of Sanchez-O'Brien Oil and Gas Company; entrepreneur John Duncan; and Bill McMinn, who was with Sterling Chemicals and had a daughter at Brookwood. I told them the story leading to the gift, and how excited we were. Then I said, "There's only one catch: we have to raise $1.1 million in endowment before they'll give us the money. So here we go again, raising money."

Suddenly, and with no hesitation or fanfare, Bill McMinn leaned over and said, "I'll give you the $1.1 million." The others all gave a loud hurrah, but I was momentarily stunned into silence, not my common response. Wow! With Bill's generous and timely commitment, we could begin construction on the Reynolds Building, which has been a tremendously effective space for us. That's the building with the five different sections under one roof.

We didn't hesitate to proceed, because the need was clearly demonstrated by our citizens and our program. We moved forward. The path became so clear in each and every step that we took. Not that we didn't continue to hit obstacles, because we did, right and left. But, as we hit one obstacle, we had learned to assess and reassess the challenge to keep working and know that answers would soon become evident. Then we'd hit another obstacle, and another opportunity would arrive. Someone has said that when you come to a corner, you don't know what is going to be around that corner but you do know Who is going to be there. The clarity with which we've been met each time we've gone around a corner or contemplated a major move has been truly amazing. We have been guided every step of the way, and those are not empty words.

God's direction became so clear in each and every step that we took.

III.

R O O T S

B rookwood grew, and we, and others, recognized it as a step toward the paradigm shift of how people with special needs are viewed. The "unteachable" were not only being taught now, but they were also holding down jobs, defining themselves as citizens, and taking pride in their productivity. They were reveling in *supervised independence.* Previously they had felt as if they were square pegs trying to fit into round holes—and Brookwood provided square holes! We had a beautiful property with well-planned buildings and safe and comfortable homes for our citizens. We had dedicated staff, a wise board, faithful volunteers and a compelling mission.

So did life become routine at this point? Heavens no! Even though we have created useful systems and successfully applied proven theories to our work, it has never become predictable or routine. We are always changing and growing, working through our challenges, sometimes with tears and sometimes with laughter. Every new citizen and every new staff member who joins us brings new gifts and new opportunities to our community. Because we are dealing with people, and everyone is unique, we are constantly learning, trying another way, adapting, and working to be the best we can be. At Brookwood, new seeds continue to be planted and many good things continue to take root, on our campus and in the lives of our citizens.

MEDICAL CARE

One of those many good things that have developed at Brookwood has been the excellent healthcare services provided to our citizens. Our first medical facility was in the old farmhouse, along with just about everything else. What is now our health center began as a modest first-aid station. As we moved into the Inn, it became a more official nurses' station. Then the time came when we needed more than a nursing station for our citizens, but how do you set up an on-site clinic? What kinds of things needed to be done?

> **One of the real God-nudges for us at Brookwood has been realizing we must seek advisors who are considered to be tops in their field.**

One of the real God-nudges for us at Brookwood has been realizing we must seek advisors who are considered to be tops in their field. We have constantly sought the finest educational advice, medical advice, nutritional advice, physical-therapy advice, and vocational advice—the finest advice in any endeavor we undertake. Then we've resolved, after determining the ways that it would be useful in our situation, to put that advice into action and to do it in good faith.

Dr. Charles Dickson, a friend of my father's, was just such an expert. He had come out to help me look for land, and he also expressed interest in helping us set up a "wellness clinic," as he called it. He just so happened to be a National Boy Scout leader and had helped establish the medical facilities used at Philmont Scout Ranch, the national Boy Scout camp in New Mexico. Dr. Dickson was certainly a well-qualified advisor in his field, and we gladly followed his recommendations.

In the beginning, as I said, we had just one nurse, Magda, working in one little room next to my office in the Inn. Then, with Dr. Dickson's guidance, we designed a clinic with two four-bed wards, two treatment rooms, offices, and a records room that you wouldn't believe. This records room is very important, because we work diligently to keep accurate and detailed medical information on each and every citizen. We are now using electronic medical records, which are very effective for us. And we have five Registered Nurses, two transporters, one scheduler, and an office manager on staff in our Health Center, serving over 200 citizens.

It was also Dr. Dickson's recommendation that we constantly research and apply new ways of delivering medical *and* dental care; he felt that such care was critically important for our citizens. So Dr. Tommy Harrison, who was at the time president of the Texas State Dental Association, came in to consult and guide us in the formation of our dental clinic. Dr. Harrison is one of those unbelievable Godsends who have helped us strive for excellence. In order to establish a cutting-edge dental clinic, we collaborated with a national sorority to provide the necessary equipment. Doctors Thomas Harrison, Douglas McClung, and Gary Williams now volunteer to work with our citizens, and, as a result, their overall dental health and hygiene has improved beyond even our expectations.

These dentists have also done a fantastic job of training our home teachers and the residential hygienists who do the "hands on" work with our citizens. The results of their efforts are amazing: Brookwood must be about the only place in the world where people are eagerly begging to go to the dentist! Our citizens love these dentists, and the dentists in turn provide them excellent care in a familiar and loving environment.

Wendy helps citizen Patricia feel better.

In establishing our Health Center, one thing we didn't want was to have a standard doctor who all of the citizens *had* to go to. Most had their own physicians who had cared for them through many years, and we didn't want to ask them to change unless they wanted to. For those who do not have a personal physician, however, we offer the services of a primary care physician, a neurologist, a podiatrist, a dermatologist, a cancer prevention specialist, a psychiatrist, a gynecologist, and an ophthalmologist. The beauty of this situation is that, instead of having to make a major change in a citizen's and staff member's day by having to pack up and go to the doctor (never a quick and easy trip), the doctors come to us. In addition to the time and effort saved, it also seems to reduce everyone's anxiety. It's been a beautiful set up.

As with every aspect of our program, medical care at Brookwood has evolved from the simplest of beginnings to an ever improving wellness clinic. Once the techniques and structures were in place, the program has continued to grow and change while keeping the essential needs of our citizens at the forefront.

> As with every aspect of our program, medical care at Brookwood has evolved from the simplest of beginnings to an ever improving wellness clinic.

A PLACE FOR WORSHIP

The year 1997 brought about the completion of the Reynolds Building. Then the Health Center was completed, and in 1998 construction began on the Worship Center and additional greenhouses. To we Brookwoodians, a place for worship is very important because we are a God-centered community. Our worship is interfaith and non-denominational, but it is central to all that we do. As you may have already guessed, everything—every building and even the grass that surrounds them—

> Everything—every building and even the grass that surrounds them—everything at The Brookwood Community has been donated.

everything at The Brookwood Community has been donated. So, let me tell you about the Worship Center and how it came to be donated.

The family of one of our citizens lived in a great neighborhood with wonderful neighbors. Among those neighbors was the Joe and Marion Mundy family. The Mundys had lived near these folks for a number of years, and saw their neighbor's son, Patrick— now a Brookwood citizen—grow up. They knew he was deaf, and they knew that the family was having a challenge trying to help him integrate into what we call "normal" society. Then Marion began to see a more enthusiastic, hopeful young man emerge, and one day she asked Patrick's mother "What is happening with Patrick?" His mother said, "We have found this wonderful place called Brookwood just west of Houston, where he has a sense of purpose and feels secure, comfortable, and very much at peace. It has made all the difference in the world in him."

That Christmas, we received a check from the Mundys (whom we didn't even know!) for $25,000. I picked up the phone and said, "My goodness! Thank you very much! Who are you? And why don't you come out and let us show you around, so that you can see what your generosity will do." They said yes and came to see us, and fortunately, became even more interested in Brookwood.

The next year, the Mundys gave us $50,000 and then $75,000 the following year. By this time, they were very deeply involved, and their interest in Brookwood had grown in meaningful ways. We went out to dinner with them one night at Christmastime and Joe handed me a little household check (not some great big thing, but a little household check) for $1 million. He said, "This is for the Worship Center." All of this began with the silent testimony of a young citizen named Patrick. His life told a story and introduced this tremendously generous family to The Brookwood Community.

When Marion and Joe gave us the funds for this vitally important building, we knew the perfect place for it—a magnificent grove of live oak trees directly in front of the main entrance. However, that is precisely where the old farmhouse was situated. That old house was a major part of our history, and we didn't want to tear it down. It was in very poor condition and beyond repair, so we made the sad decision to let it go. That was very traumatic for those of us who had worked in it for years. But what went up in its place is even more special to us.

The Worship Center that the Mundys's gift provided is now the centerpiece of Brookwood. In addition to being used for our official worship services, it is also a place for meetings and for weddings. Each year many couples who want a beautiful wedding venue and who wish to support our citizens choose to marry at Brookwood. Our Worship Center also provides work opportunities for our citizens. It is a vitally important part of our community.

(Left) Dave, John, and Rosemary resisting the tractor.
(Right) Raising the steeple.

The Mundys have been major benefactors for us over the years, and still are. Joe has passed on, but Marion has stayed true to the colors. Many, many people are eternally grateful for, and have greatly benefited from, the Mundys's involvement in Brookwood. Their generosity has touched thousands of lives in meaningful ways.

We dedicated the Worship Center at the twentieth anniversary of the first citizens joining Brookwood. And for that dedication ceremony, we had some wonderful guests on hand. I would call them VIPs, but all Brookwoodians are VIPs, so that term wouldn't work here. One of these famous guests was Barbara Bush (again–thank goodness for Barbara Bush!), and also Pastor Kirbyjon Caldwell of Houston's Windsor Village United Methodist Church. It was a big event, and since Barbara Bush was with us, we went through a detailed Secret Service briefing. They told us what we could and could not do and advised that there would be lots of security in and around the Worship Center where we planned to have the ceremony.

The dedication ceremony was well underway and going beautifully when all of a sudden one of our citizens, Margaret, jumped up, ran down the middle aisle of the Worship Center, climbed the stairs, grabbed hold of Mrs. Bush, and hugged her, again and again. Then Margaret turned around and walked back to her seat.

I looked at the Secret Service men who were there in the church, and prayed "Oh Lord, please, don't let them shoot her!" They looked as surprised as we were! Spontaneous hugging must not be covered in their service manual. Fortunately, they did the right thing, as usual. They may or may not have known that Margaret had grown up knowing Barbara Bush; her parents and the Bushes had been friends since both couples lived in Midland many years ago, and it had been her parents who suggested we invite Mrs. Bush to the first dedication ceremony. It was one of those instances I'm sure no one who witnessed will ever forget. In addition to Margaret's enthusiastic greeting, the ceremony was lovely; the church was full, and Barbara and Kirbyjon were, as always, their brilliant selves.

WORSHIP AT BROOKWOOD

The stained-glass windows in our Worship Center represent products that we make or grow in our community, and these beautiful windows were given in honor of parents, citizens, and friends. On our altar, a cross and a menorah sit comfortably together. At Brookwood, we are more concerned with what we have in common than what our differences are, but we honor and enjoy the differences also. If you want to experience that ecumenical spirit, I invite you to come to one of our worship services. Unofficial and official worship takes on many forms in our community. Our

> We are more concerned with what we have in common than what our differences are, but we honor and enjoy the differences also.

"unofficial" worship goes on all the time and our "official" worship takes place on Sundays. Some of our citizens attend Sunday morning services at local churches in nearby Brookshire. Others go to our very informal and enjoyable three o'clock afternoon service in the Worship Center. Then from time to time we have the "church on wheels"—an idea that I think is just brilliant.

Some of our folks who are more severely involved get on the bus, and they are driven around on Sunday mornings, going past nearby churches. When they spot a church, the bus stops there on the street and gets the name of that church. Then everybody on the bus cheers, "Yay, God! Hurray for God!" If they are not able to speak they may just clap, and then they move on to the next church. It is a wonderful way for these citizens to take time from their work week to acknowledge the presence of God and a reminder that worship looks different for all of us.

A number of our citizens don't do well at the formal churches outside of our Brookwood community. On one occasion, a citizen made an appointment to talk with me. When she came in she said, "Mrs. Streit, I have a complaint to make."

I said, "Well, all right. What is it?"

"They won't let me go to church any more. And I need to go to church."

I thought, "My golly. What's going on here?" So I asked, "Well, why can't you go to church anymore?"

"I don't know. It's just Greg and all of those people decided that I should not go to church anymore."

> **The pastor told Greg, "I don't think she's ready for church yet."**

I assured her we would put that complaint into God's jar—I will explain about "God's jar" a little later—and told her that I would investigate her complaint.

I checked with Greg Glauser, our Spiritual and Citizen Life Director, and he explained to me what had happened. Greg and several Brookwood citizens had gone to a church in Brookshire, and the preacher was talking about how important it is to help people. Someone always helps us, he said, and we're always thankful when they do.

When this citizen heard this, she jumped up, stood on the pew (she was quite short) and said, "Well, the Brookwood staff sure as hell doesn't help me!" (Please understand that we try not to use profanity at Brookwood at *any* time, much less at church.) "They make me dress myself," she went on, "and they make me be sure and take a shower! And they make me eat things I don't want to eat–stuff they call healthy! And then they make me go to the clinic when something might be wrong, just to check it out! And there's no need for that! So you see, they sure don't help me!"

Well, Greg said they got her to sit down, but when they walked out, the minister suggested maybe she wasn't really ready for church yet, and it would be better if she didn't come back.

When I discovered what had happened, we put her on a little sabbatical and explained the expectations at that church. She decided that she wanted to attend that church and would work to do better. She was eventually able to go again. She now understands that, some of the rules of *regular* worship are not the same as the rules that we have at Brookwood worship. At Brookwood, people may wander around, leave to go to the bathroom, or decide to leave. I overheard one citizen saying when he passed me as he was walking down the aisle, "I don't like that song so I'm outta here!" I remember thinking to myself, "I've felt that way too," but I just didn't say it out loud. At Brookwood—even in worship—you learn to expect the unexpected.

> ## At Brookwood—even in worship—you learn to expect the unexpected.

GOD'S JAR AND GOD'S CHAIR

I mentioned God's jar—and it plays a special role at Brookwood. We have a jar in each studio, and I always have a jar on my desk. If Brookwoodians come to me with a problem, whether they are sad or frustrated, or they have a complaint of some kind, we write their problem down and put it in the jar. This is our symbolic way of giving our troubles to God. Putting whatever it might be in God's jar just seems to help us move on. It's been a very good, therapeutic solution to some of our problems, because often those problems placed in the jar will be forgotten—and that's probably God working on our memory and helping us to let go. When we give whatever

God's chair.

is troubling us away to God, we say in effect, "Now. He's got it, and I can let go of it." It takes an effort not to think of it again, but together we can remind each other that we've put that concern in God's jar, and it's *His* problem now. Because He likes to take care of our problems, we can take ourselves out of it. That doesn't mean that we don't do what we can to help each other

> We give whatever is troubling us away to God.

and ourselves, but God's jar really helps us understand that God cares and that He will take care of it.

So God's jar helps us to be always aware of His presence with us. Like any family, we live together with the same challenges and joys that intimacy brings. We work together, we play together, and we break bread together. One thing that makes it all work for us is that we make sure to always save a visible place for God. He is always present with us, as the jar reminds us, but let me tell you how he actually got a chair.

Many years ago, one of our citizens came to me and said, "You know what Mrs. Streit? We talk about God all the time, and we know He's here, even though we can't see Him. And we're glad He's here. But do you know what bothers me? We don't have a place for Him to sit, and I think God deserves a place to sit at Brookwood."

We thought, "Well, why not? We'll get a special chair and place it strategically around the campus so that our citizens will know that that is God's chair, and it will represent His presence in this place. So God has a chair in the classrooms, another in the cafetorium, one in the visitors' center, and certainly one in the Worship Center. When we put God's chair in the Worship Center, one of our citizens came forward and in a loud voice said, "I'm glad we put a chair here because it is very approximate." I think that he meant appropriate, but he was close.

Not everyone who visits Brookwood knows about God's chair, however. One day the chancel choir of a local church came to sing at our three o'clock service. They sang beautifully, and when they stopped singing, some choir members were visiting with our citizens. One of the older choir members went over and sat down in the empty chair—God's chair. Virginia, one of our senior citizens walked up onto the stage, leaned over, and in what sounded like a stage whisper said, "Do you know you're sitting in *God's chair?*"

The confused lady jumped up, and then Virginia said to her, "Oh, never mind. It's okay. He won't mind." I'm sure He wouldn't have, either—but the lady never did sit back down in that chair, or any other chair that day.

WORLD CLASS DINING IN BROOKSHIRE

The Café at Brookwood has become a favorite spot for guests and one of the busiest places on our campus each day between eleven and two o'clock. Fortunately, and unfortunately, I eat often at our Café. I love it, but it just may be responsible for an extra pound or two. My favorite things on the menu are the Chicken Crepes Contessa, the Fried Eggplant Stacker, the Mahi Mahi, and the Turkey, Avocado, and Bacon Club Sandwich—plus about a dozen other delicious items. I try not to eat the desserts even though they are "to die for," because my body doesn't need any more company. But the most important thing about our Café is not the fabulous food, it's that it is a great place of employment for our citizens. They do not work in food preparation, but they have numerous other necessary jobs. We have a crew of citizens that arrive about 9:00 a.m. each day to set up the tables, put the tablecloths on them, roll up the napkins with silverware inside, fix the centerpieces, and do whatever else has to be done to make our Café first class. Then the servers come to get dressed in their uniforms and prepare to work with their teachers to take drink orders and serve our patrons. Another crew will fill the salt and pepper shakers, place crackers in their serving containers, and do the same for the sugar and sweeteners. Our citizens have varied gifts, and those gifts fit the various jobs in the Café. All the work is important, and every task requires unique skills and talents.

> **The most important thing about our Café is not the fabulous food, it's that it is a great place of employment for our citizens.**

As important as our Café is to Brookwood today, it was not a part of our community for several years. Although when we visited Lambs Farm in the late 1970s we had seen a very nice tearoom operating there, a restaurant didn't seem feasible at Brookwood at that time. That all changed in 1999.

Early that year, we received a call from a woman who was in charge of planning excursions for the many conventions coming into Houston. One of those—the World Energy Council—was coming to the United States for the first time and meeting in Houston. The woman who called was arranging activities for the delegates' spouses, and she wanted to bring them to Brookwood. Of course we were thrilled to death that they would choose us, and we began to talk about what such a visit would entail. "Now, we're going to want a place to eat," she said, and I replied that Brookshire had some perfectly fine places to eat, and Katy did, as well.

"No! No, no, no," she said. "We don't want to eat at some *ordinary* place, we want to eat with you at *your* place."

I thought, "Oh, my golly." We really wanted the honor of having the World Energy Council executives' wives visit Brookwood—that was so important—but we didn't have a place for them to eat. Was this another nudge from God saying, "It's time to address that tearoom idea?" This was in March, and I asked her, "Well, when are you planning to come?"

She said, "We're not coming until October."

"Oh, yes," I said. "That will be just fine. We can accommodate you here on campus." And that was the beginning of the Café. After all, eight months is plenty of time to develop and launch a restaurant, right?

Normally, the administrative staff brought our own lunches to work and sat at a table in the supply room to eat, but we occasionally went out. There were only two places to eat in Brookshire that we all liked. One was a truck stop and the other was a restaurant called The Cotton Gin. The Cotton Gin had a great salad bar and served delicious small loaves of homemade bread, and all of the food was really good. Then a sad thing happened and the restaurant closed. This proved to be an opportunity for us, however, and the timing was perfect. We knew we had the green light on starting a restaurant, and of course we had to find a chef. Because we all liked the food at The Cotton Gin, I called Laura, the chef who had been working there, and asked her if she would like to come to Brookwood and start the Café with us. She was very talented and had studied at the Culinary Institute of America in Hyde Park, New York. I thought that she was going to come through the phone she was so excited. We had a tasting committee to help find recipes we thought would sell, and she tried them out on us. She passed with flying colors.

At the time we had a large commercial kitchen in the Inn. It was set up to prepare thirty-four breakfasts and dinners each day for the citizens who lived there. The citizens ate their lunches in the large lunchroom in another building, which was closer to their work, so that freed up the kitchen for us to use for lunch. This meant that we had usable space—all we had to do was to get the proper tables and chairs and upgrade the kitchen a bit. Everything came together quite well, and we planned a wonderful menu for our guests, taught a few of our citizens how to take drink orders and serve lunch with the supervision of teachers, and we were ready for the big day.

We had a dry run the day before our European guests were to arrive, and if you've ever seen an example of total failure, that was it. From the "unique" tablecloths to the rickety tables, to the fact that we burned the entrée, dropped plates, and spilled water—it was all a mess. Everything you could have possibly imagined went wrong. But the next day, you know what? It was great. It could not have been better.

And all of these ladies enjoyed it immensely; at least, they acted like they did. We weren't able to converse with them because none had been to the United States before, only two spoke broken English, and we didn't speak their languages, either. But they were happy, they saw our people working really hard, and they loved the food, and that's what counted. This celebrity visit to Brookwood thrust us towards our present-day Café, which now serves nearly 1,000 people per week.

Each day brings many opportunities to adjust and adapt.

As anyone who has run a restaurant can attest, serving food day in and day out is quite an adventure—and it has certainly been so for us. Each day brings many opportunities to adjust and adapt—like the day chef Laura, called in with 103° F temperature and thought she had the flu. She really didn't think it would be a good idea for her to come run the kitchen, and we said we didn't think it would be a good idea either.

Even though we had a big group coming that day (big in those days was forty or so people), we said "Don't worry, we can handle it." When the line cooks in the kitchen found out Laura wasn't going to be there, they turned to us and said "We weren't hired to do that kind of work, so we are leaving." And just like that, they walked out.

Well, there we were, not knowing what to do either. But we were all in it together. We were used to having to adapt and be flexible, so that's what we did. It took Joe Mazzu—our development director who happened to be a gourmet cook—and Sylvia Patton, our dedicated assistant director who is a champion organizer, to get the show on the road. The food was already prepped, but it did need to be cooked. They sent me out to Sam's Club to buy desserts; I think in order to get rid of me. Somehow, we served the group that came. Evidently they were happy, because they've come back many, many times since then. But you know what? Those workers who walked out on us that day never did come back, and our Café is still going strong.

Teacher assisting Frank with taking drink selections.

The Café is not only a great place for visitors, and a wonderful employment opportunity for our citizens, but also it has actually become a revenue producing enterprise. Another special windfall from the Café came when Dr. Gary Mesibov, a friend of Briarwood and Brookwood and one of our valued educational experts came to visit us. Dr. Mesibov is Professor Emeritus at the University of North Carolina, Chapel Hill, where he taught for over thirty-five years. He came to observe how we have adapted his TEACCH program in our work with adults. When he came, he was amazed and very gratified to see his principles adapted and in operation every-where—in our lunchroom, classrooms, homes, studios, and enterprises.

While he was in Houston, a group of parents hosted a lovely dinner for Dr. Mesibov, and at that dinner, they served a salad with a *wonderful* salad dressing. The dressing was so delicious that, with its creator's permission, we took the recipe back to our Café, where it became an instant hit. People asked for more of the special dressing time and again, and we gladly sent small Styrofoam cups of it home with them. Soon the requests grew so frequent that we started bottling it by hand, and selling it! When demand quickly outstripped our old-fashioned bottling method, we decided to try to get someone to give us some bottling equipment. The Paul Newman Foundation indicated their interest and asked how we were currently bot-tling the dressing. "With a pitcher and a funnel," we told them, and they laughed. Then they gave us some simple yet effective bottling equipment.

In honor of Dr. Mesibov's many contributions to the life of our citi-zens—and his visit that serendipitously launched this product—we call it "Mesibov Dressing." Today, it is sold at our stores, and at HEB, a major, family-owned food store chain headquartered in Texas and a great friend of Brookwood. Dr. Mesibov was at Brookwood again not long ago, and he said, "You know, I used to be known for my work with autistic children; now I'm more famous for my salad dressing—which I don't even know how to make!"

THE BROOKWOOD STORE

I remember years ago one of our volunteers would say to me in a very quiet and unassuming whisper, "We need a store." A few days or weeks later she would quietly say again, "Yvonne—we need a store." This hap-pened more times than you can imagine, so the idea of a store was always very much alive but under the radar. I guess those persistent words, to-gether with our crafts program and our aspiring citizens finally drove the point home. So, eventually, we got busy and built a store. Situated out by the horticulture center, it was a little log cabin, made possible by the gifts of several donors. Good friends who owned a very successful retail store came out after the store was finished and decorated it for us. In two days, they did what it usually takes about two weeks to accomplish. We literally had boxes everywhere when they came in one morning, and the next day was to be our grand opening. We were scared to death—we didn't know what to do with all the things we had, or how to make them appealing. But they did. They worked like beavers to get that store ready and make it look appealing and rustic. We christened it the Sherren Smith Gift & Garden Center, in memory of Randy and Ann Smith's daughter who had worked for us in the farmhouse.

The location for that first store was not good, and consequently we did not attract people from the highway—or any other place for that matter. Even though we sold a lot of our plants there, we made very little money, and some months we didn't quite break even. Although we didn't realize it at the time, what might have been a good-sized mistake for us became instead another "failing forward."

Then, on October 27, 2000, our store burned down. The shop was totally destroyed, but the blaze occurred late in the evening when no one was inside. The response from our local volunteer firefighters was swift and efficient. A neighbor saw the flames and called the Brookshire Volunteer Fire Department, who responded within minutes. They, along with the Katy and Fulshear Volunteer Fire Departments, worked for hours to keep the fire contained, saving the attached greenhouse and the shade structure behind the store. Thankfully, the fire did not reach any other buildings. To this day, the cause is still unknown.

After this loss, two churches put out the call to their congregations. Each church responded with major gifts to begin the "fire fund," enabling us to re-open a bigger and better store, which, throughout the ensuing years, has provided a major portion of our revenue. We consider members of these and other churches who offered their prayers and support to be part of "God's construction team" and they made miracles happen.

Our citizens learned of the fire the next day, but fortunately, seventy-five volunteers from a large Houston bank were on campus for a fall celebration, and that activity took their minds off the fire. Their home teachers and the activities staff reassured citizens of their safety, and turned discussions away from the fire by talking about new opportunities.

One group of citizens asked their teacher how we could sell things that we make when we didn't even have a store. A suggestion from another citizen was for everyone to buy a lottery ticket and not let anyone else win the jackpot. We couldn't quite figure out how we could do that, so that suggestion was discarded. Then the citizens became excited about the possibility of rebuilding, and one asked if we could find donors that might build a mall to go with our new store. "If they build a mall for us, do you think they'd put in a movie theater with popcorn?" Remember, Brookwood citizens think big.

Brookwood citizens think big.

Within a day, however, employees and volunteers had erected a tent, and we re-opened for business with plenty of product on hand. The "fire fund" helped offset our expenses over and above what was covered by insurance. Friends supported us after this loss in so many ways, and we were so grateful. With the support of our donors, many helping hands, and God's leadership, we knew that we would recover from this terrible blow.

And there is one other thing I should tell you about the fire: once the smoke had cleared, only one piece of product was left that was identifiable. Hanging on a charred wall was a manger-scene plaque, with an angel leaning over the roof of the manger, looking down at Mary and the baby Jesus. The message it seemed to send was, *Don't worry. I'm still here!*

We began planning a new store almost immediately with the fire fund. We hired an architect and contacted our all-star builder, Louis Gaeke, and before long the new building was underway. This time we were on a very visible prime location on campus. With about 5,000 square feet of store space, a retail green house, a garden area to display plants and a beautiful waterfall, it was more than we could have imagined only a few months before. Then, in 2010, we added another 4,000 square feet to the store to display products made by the artisans of Brookwood as well as market items, Shudde Bros. western hats, and a selection of art for our fine art gallery. Today's store is gorgeous and its proceeds help to underwrite the operating costs of The Brookwood Community and all of its citizens.

The enterprises we had struggled so long to find and worked so hard to teach the citizens are now contributing 40% of our annual budget. Most importantly, as we always dreamed, they are providing our citizens with purpose and self esteem. We firmly believe that if we become more efficient in the control of expenses, more exceptional in the design and production of handcrafted products and in horticulture, our enterprises could contribute even more substantially to the support of this mission. Many of our initial attempts lost money either because they were too costly to produce or the products themselves lacked a ready market. Through a process of trial and error in addition to determination and persistence we came to a balance of products our citizens could produce, enjoy producing and that consumers wanted to buy. The progress toward the goal of becoming self –sustaining is making great strides while providing opportunities for our citizens to contribute to society in a meaningful way. But no matter how self-sustaining we become, we are always aware of our interdependence as a community. We could never have come this far without God's grace and the generosity of his angels on Earth.

> No matter how self-sustaining we become, we are always aware of our interdependence as a community.

BROOKWOOD VOLUNTEERS

From the beginning, Brookwood has been blessed with generous and numerous volunteers. In our early years, we didn't have enough teachers, and we didn't really know how to integrate new citizens into the community as well as we do now, so the extra hands and hearts of our volunteers saved the day on many occasions. We are still learning minute-by-minute and day-by-day at Brookwood, and whatever the new discoveries we have made about curriculum or the practicalities of creating community with people with different abilities are, our volunteers have always been important partners in the work. We are so thankful for the way they bring God's love to life. They may assist our citizens in how to hold a sponge to do sponge painting, or how to keep within the lines of a glazed ornament, or how to be gentle when planting, or just about anything. Their presence has been a constant gift to us from day one.

It's hard to really get people to understand the significance of having a dedicated volunteer group. We are so very indebted to the volunteers who began with us and who are still doing their part—and more—to help further the cause of the Brookwood Community. For instance, when we first started the store, it was staffed entirely by volunteers. We didn't have any paid employees at this retail outlet and the only products that we had were the things we had made. We wanted the products to be so good that folks would think for sure that we got them at one of the upscale gift markets all over this country. But we weren't there yet. So the volunteers came to our rescue again. They made place mats and hand-painted hand towels. These beautiful items added beauty and interest to our inventory. These great friends served as retail staff, provided hospitality, increased our revenues, and quite literally made that store run!

Before we had our own pool in the Reynolds Building, volunteers would help our citizens go to a neighborhood pool to swim on hot summer days. They also helped with field trips, sponged ornaments, cut patterns, washed windows, held picnics, conducted tours when we had them and performed dozens of "other duties as assigned." Their efforts made it possible for each and every Brookwood citizen to have a better life, and that is a monumental statement.

So much of America runs on volunteerism.

Today, our volunteers do some of the same tasks, but their roles are a bit different now than they were in the farmhouse days, because of the size of our community and staff. Volunteers still generously do whatever needs to be done, but as our work has become more defined, so have their roles. For example, volunteer tour guides now come five days a week to act as docents in introducing visitors to our community, and theirs is a critical role. It takes an awful lot of effort to study what we're trying to do and express it well to the variety of groups who regularly come to tour.

Our volunteers are smart, and they are loyal. I noticed this past Christmas, Carol, the first person to volunteer when we moved out to the country was—and still is—one of our number one "general flunkies." In our community, the term general flunky is a highly complimentary title! This real can-do helper came with the first group of volunteers who ever enriched our program, and she has been with us almost thirty years. It's wonderful to see how consistent the love of our volunteers has been.

So much of America runs on volunteerism. This outstanding group of people hasn't limited their efforts to consistent gifts of labor and expertise, either. They help us to raise money for the community as well. Some time ago, our volunteers organized a luncheon featuring outstanding speakers who would appeal to the business community, as well as draw attention to the mission of Brookwood.

One such luncheon featured a former big league pitcher, Dave Dravecky, a remarkable man, as our speaker. Dave really knew what it was like to have special challenges. He had had cancer in his pitching arm, had the tumor removed, and had diligently worked his way through rehabilitation and back to pitching. Then, during his comeback game the following season, Dave threw "the pitch heard round the world," and his pitching arm snapped in two. The cancer had returned and Dave had to have his arm, shoulder blade, and collarbone amputated. He gave a terrific talk at our luncheon, and was an inspiring example of grace. Afterward, as I was talking with him, one of our citizens, Jason, came rushing up. He looked up at Dave and at his empty sleeve and asked him, "What happened to your arm?"

Dave said, "Well, I had cancer, and I had to have them take my arm off so that the cancer wouldn't get to the rest of my body."

"Well, okay—but where is your arm?" the citizen asked again.

Dave said, "Well, I don't have it any more."

"Well I know that—but *where is it?*" Jason wanted to know where that arm was *right now.*

Dave said without missing a beat, "You know, it's a secret. It's hiding some place." And that explanation was okay with the young man, who went right on his way.

Dave was just super about our citizen's questioning. In fact he said, "I really enjoy the direct openness of these folks—it is so refreshing." Dave talked about living with a disability and how other people can help you face that challenge. He talked about his teammates and how much they meant to him during his battle with cancer, and after. He talked about how that same kind of teamwork is exemplified at Brookwood; and he quoted Andrew Carnegie, who said:

"Teamwork is the fuel that allows common people to attain uncommon results." This wonderful saying ties in with another from Margaret Meade who said, "Don't tell me that a small group of dedicated, resourceful people can't change the world because, indeed, that is all who have."Over time, I've learned never to underestimate the passion, sense of purpose, and persistence of Brookwood volunteers, both on our campus, and in the greater community. One of our early volunteers decided that garage sales might be a way for us to raise some extra money. To prove her point, she jumped in to hold one in her neighborhood—one of the Memorial Villages. She knew that garage sales are not allowed in the Villages, but she wasn't going to let that little detail deter her plan. She enlisted several other determined parents to help her, and they set up a huge garage sale in her backyard. She told everybody what their assigned positions were for the day of the sale, and what time they should arrive. The night before she put up signs announcing the backyard sale to begin at 7:30 the next morning. That time "happened" to coincide with the Village police shift change, and she figured they would be busy for an hour or so after that, which would give her a head start. Sure enough, about 9:00 a.m., here came the police—and she was ready. She was never without a well-thought-out plan.

> **"Teamwork is the fuel that allows common people to attain uncommon results."**

She knew that she was going to have to get them to be sympathetic to the cause, and that perhaps she might win them over by telling stories and asking advice. So she told them about her daughter who lived at Brookwood, and she had pictures of her daughter and all of the other workers' children who lived there. She explained how very important it was for these citizens that this sale happen. One of her great gifts was the ability to make small talk, and her delaying tactics were beyond compare. She asked the officers if they had children, and if they worked to give their children a better life; what school did their children attend, how old were they, and did they have any pets? Then she pointed to her car in the garage and mentioned it had something wrong with it and her husband didn't know anything about cars. She asked if they thought it could be fixed, and if not, she wondered what kind of car that they thought she ought to buy. She talked about everything that you could think of and some things you wouldn't, and when she described her daughter she teared up because her daughter was so happy at this wonderful new place—and thankful that *all* (spreading her arms out wide toward the other volunteers) of these friends out of the goodness of their hearts came from across town to help with this endeavor! Then one at a time she asked the volunteers to come over and meet these nice officers who she *knew* truly wanted to help, but had some sticky rule that might make them have to close it down—all the time not even pausing between sentences. The officers were too polite to interrupt.

She gave the officers cookies and coffee and invited them to come back and have breakfast the next morning. I truly don't know all of the shenanigans she went through to try to get these very nice policemen to relent and let the garage sale go on—but her performance was "Lucy and Ethel" good. When she finally took a breath the nice officers told her how sorry they were that they had to ask her to close, but that they would be back later and expected her to have closed up by the time they got back. Well, they didn't ever come back and Brookwood got almost $1,800 from that sale—and believe me it was like a gift from above.

The moral of this story? Never underestimate the love and persistence of a Brookwood volunteer!

**Never underestimate the love and persistence
of a Brookwood volunteer!**

GREEN AND GROWING THINGS

The successes and failures we've had at Brookwood growing things— from pine trees and Valentine-settias (more on this later) to jasmine cuttings and pansies, poinsettias and more—have far outweighed the few horticultural misses we've experienced along the way—like hydroponic tomatoes. Growing *anything* is a good example of how our "practical education in tandem with life" philosophy provides citizens with opportunities for success beyond our wildest dreams. One year, we planted pansies, dianthus, and snapdragons in our greenhouses, and they were just gorgeous. We had all of these wonderful, lovingly and laboriously planted flowers, and we expected the Houston winter to be comparatively mild, with low temperatures of 28° F at most. We put the cold hardy plants from the greenhouses outside where we believed they would be safe. We had these plants all over the place. Then, lo and behold, we got a forecast we couldn't believe—it was going to go down to 17° F and then get no higher than the low 20s for the next few days. Oh, my golly! Steve, our horticulturist, went nuts, because he knew how much the seedlings, the pots, and the soil, had cost—not to mention the overwhelming amount of labor that had gone into teaching our citizens to plant all those plants. We were at risk of losing that hard-won investment of time, money, and effort.

What could we do with all of those plants—at least a thousand of them— that we had so laboriously planted? This was *not* supposed to happen in Houston! Our citizens could see that the staff was very concerned about saving the plants. Chad, one of our citizens, came up to Steve and in very garbled but intense words gave him definite instructions, the same words that Chad's father always told him: "Don't be upset—just use your head."

Steve stopped, looked at Chad, and said to himself that that might be a very good idea. With creativity and determination we sprang into action. We had some shade cloth and some beat-up poles; and, with these, we put up a temporary cover to hold whatever heat there might be near the ground, hoping it would provide protection for a few of our precious plants.

Then came the challenge of getting *many* flats of seedling plants moved under our ad-hoc structure. *All* of the staff—and I mean the cook, the nurse, the teachers, the secretary, the administrative staff, and the citizens moved those plants, and it was *oh so cold*. We sang songs and talked about hot chocolate and counted the minutes until we could get some with marsh-mallows in it. With that kind of encouragement we got the job done. But, the question remained: would it work?

When the freeze was over, the plants on the edges of the shade struc-ture died, but most of the others survived. And all of the plants in the greenhouses made it through the freeze. This was a great bonding moment for all of us, and we realized that we should always be on the lookout for opportunities to nurture this teamwork.

We were not so lucky, however, with our hydroponic tomatoes.

Some of our ideas work beyond our wildest dreams and some fall on their face, but we are willing to give each of them 100% effort. One of these ideas was growing hydroponic tomatoes. The CEO of one of the ma-jor food market chains in Houston was promoting hydroponic vegetables for his wonderful food stores and had come out to Brookwood. He had been very impressed with what our citizens could do in the horti-culture area. He said, "If you grow hydro-ponic tomatoes, we'll buy them from you. I'll

> Some of our ideas work beyond our wildest dreams and some fall on their face, but we are willing to give each of them 100% effort.

provide the boxes, and we'll take care of the pick-up and delivery." We thought, "Oh, my golly. That sounds wonderful. Let's look into that."

We like to consult with experts, so off I went to Texas A&M University, just up the road in College Station, to confer with their horticulture depart-ment about the chance of success of such a venture. They threw us a curve because they said that the Gulf Coast area was not conducive to growing tomatoes hydroponically. Well that was *not* what I wanted to hear, so I decided to get a second opinion. We were told that Kansas State University had a good horticulture division, too, so we set up a telephone appointment and consulted with them—same answer.

Well, I thought, those university folks just didn't know how hard we work, or that we are so determined that we can make difficult things happen. So in my hardheaded brilliance, in *spite* of my firm belief that experience is the best teacher and the knowledge that A&M and Kansas State had experience, I said, "Let's go with it. We can do it!" We got started, and we had tomatoes, tomatoes, and tomatoes. They grew tall, and then the vines would "take off" across the lines that we had elevated and strung across the entire greenhouse. Those tomatoes were beautiful. But there was one problem: in order to make a profit, the clusters of tomatoes needed to grow about three feet apart. Our clusters were growing a *minimum* of five feet apart. We have too many overcast days in Houston, and tomatoes need full sun for more days than we normally have. Consequently, we were producing about *half* of the tomatoes we needed to grow to make a profit.

The folks at the grocery stores we were working with were really trying to help us, but there was not much any of us could do about the weather. So hydroponic tomatoes were something of a flop, but we may try again if some brilliant horticulturist can come up with a tomato that thrives on overcast days. We also learned that yes, it is a good idea to seek advice from experts, but sometimes you need to pay attention to what they say! In the meantime, the tomato greenhouses have been adapted to be a home for poinsettias, hanging baskets, and geraniums—and those *are* thriving.

Transferring poinsettias to larger pots.

A year or two earlier, while I was still working at Briarwood, Rosemary and I went on one of our research trips to consult with a couple of people in Hawkins, Texas. While we were driving back to Houston, we accidentally found greenhouses *full* of poinsettias. We brought twenty-four of the plants back in my station wagon and began investigating whether or not we could grow them in our four little greenhouses. The consultants we talked to were very discouraging, however. They told us that if the plants were exposed to any light during a certain ten- to eleven-hour period of time in their growth cycle, they wouldn't turn red. Also, they are a fragile plant and very brittle, they are difficult to plant, and they must be carefully spaced out. Bottom line: they didn't think we could or should try growing them at Brookwood.

After seeking encouragement from consultants who were experts in this field for about three or four years (and who discouraged this idea), we decided, in spite of our "advice experience" with hydroponic tomatoes, "Hey, you know what, we think we can do this, so let's just try. We can kind of watch out and keep the headlights of cars away, and we're secluded, so maybe it would work." We planted an experimental crop of maybe 200 poinsettias. Sure enough, lights got to the crop, and they didn't bloom until *February*. So we decided, "Oh well, we'll try to sell them as Valentine-settias." And our sweet parents came along and bought them, as did some of our neighbors.

We learned a valuable lesson, and today, we have learned to grow and sell more poinsettias than you can imagine. During the 2015 Christmas season we sold 46,000 of them to churches, corporations, and individuals. Our citizens planted each and every one of them, helped space them, helped put the fertilizer drip-system together, took them over to our retail greenhouse (yes, we were able to keep the lights off of them), and went on deliveries to help unload. We've got some

> **Behind those plants are the hands and hearts of our citizens.**

incredible friends, churches, and corporations who buy poinsettias from us year after year, and say they're the prettiest poinsettias they've ever seen. And of course we think so, too, but here again, we're just slightly biased.

The success of our horticulture enterprise is not just about plants. Behind those plants are the hands and hearts of our citizens. When I first started wearing my red smock and working with Vicki years ago, we were just trying to get her to respond to commands. When we came out to Brookwood, she learned to put individual pots in flats utilizing that tactile kinesthetic method that Dr. Kephart had discovered to be her asset avenue of learning at Purdue. By 1987, she put *11,000 pots* into flats in one year. When I heard she had done that, it took me back to those early days and the thousands of times we repeated, "grasp, lift, place, and release." It had finally paid off. Vicki felt good about it, and she certainly contributed to our horticulture venture. She's still working in horticulture and still enjoying it. She's part of a very diverse team, and because of creative, diligent, and determined teachers she and all her fellow citizens have learned how to make better use of their abilities to make things grow at Brookwood—plants and people alike.

Like everything at Brookwood, the poinsettia program grew over time. When we first started planting them, all of the administrative staff had to go down to the greenhouses and plant. We would stand there nearly all day in the August heat, putting fragile baby poinsettias plants into four-inch pots. Working with the citizens was fun, productive, and another important bonding experience. As time went on, the citizens began to be more confident and competent, and they wanted to do it on their own. Finally, all the administrative staff got *kicked out.* Now our citizens do all of the planting and spacing on their own. They are justifiably proud of their accomplishment.

> **Citizens have learned how to make better use of their abilities to make things grow at Brookwood—plants and people alike.**

They are also proud of each other, because they understand that they are part of a team. Once Vicki gets the pots in the flats, the next step is filling the pots with soil. Because a lot of the dirt that was supposed to go into the pots landed on the floor, we realized the need for a semi-automated pot-filler, which was a great improvement. Our citizens really thought they were "big time" when they loaded the soil into the machine and then fed the flats through it and the pots came out loaded. Wow!

John, one of our citizens who was working at the machine, whooped and hollered when he saw that first flat come through with soil neatly deposited in every pot. His teacher said, "Hey John, I think you like the way that machine works."

And John said, "I was just glad that the pots didn't get eaten." He was tickled, and we had the privilege of seeing that amazing scene though his delighted eyes—another reason we celebrate neurodiversity at Brookwood!

We celebrate neurodiversity at Brookwood!

LEARNING TO TEACH, AND TEACHING TO LEARN

From the beginning, teaching has been integral to the Brookwood experience. We've collectively spent decades doing research, visiting other excellent programs, learning best practices, and adapting the techniques we have learned to benefit our very special citizens. Learning never stops at Brookwood—for our staff, or for

> **Learning never stops at Brookwood—for our staff, or for our citizens.**

our citizens. Discoveries in learning and adapting happen daily, and we share what we have learned with others.

Rita and Christi reading her communication board.

I've already told you how important Dr. Kephart's work has been to Brookwood, and a little about the TEACCH program of Dr. Gary Mesibov. We have also used Dr. Marc Gold's teaching techniques throughout our entire history. Dr. Gold did his work at the University of Illinois at Urbana-Champaign in the 1960s, authoring a book called *Try Another Way*. He believed that disabled people are best served by being trained in market-able skills, and that persons labeled as disabled respond best when treated with respect for their worth and competence. He was a strong proponent of observation as a basis for finding the most effective way of teaching each individual. Perhaps you can imagine how that resonated with me because of my firm belief in the power of observation. As I've said before, observation helps a good teacher become great when they find out how a person learns best—is it through their visual avenue, through their auditory, or tactile or motor avenue or all of the above?

If you can teach a competency to someone, your awareness of his or her deviances will seem to fade away.

Dr. Gold also spoke of the competence deviance theory—that is, if you can teach a competency to someone, your awareness of his or her devianc-es will seem to fade away. Our citizens felt the pride of accomplishment in their developing competencies, and this made the ways they differed, their deviances, seem less noticeable. Therefore, a stranger who might meet this citizen would be so amazed at the accomplishment of a task that the citi-zen's deviancies would become less prominent. Instead of being hesitant to talk to that citizen, the stranger would find himself or herself saying, "My goodness, how on earth did you learn to do that?"

Dr. Gold also had another theory—a small but important teaching tech-nique. He was a great proponent of being on an equal physical level with whomever you were teaching. As an example, he never would *stand* beside someone who was *sitting*—to teach that person, he sat beside her. In most cases after he had determined the student's asset avenue of learning, which was usually visual, he did not talk to them, because he felt that the verbal input added clutter to the teaching situation. He would get eye contact as much as possible, and then would get his eyes to go to the project. By doing that, the student's eyes went to the project, too, and consequently her attention would follow.

Dr. Gold demonstrates this theory in a film called "Try Another Way" that I believe can still be viewed on the Internet. In it, a forty-two-year old man is seen assembling a bicycle brake, a task that probably neither you nor I could do without proper training. Oddly enough, the man in the film had a 42 IQ, so to assemble that bicycle brake was an amazing feat. A group of people touring the workshop clearly did not know how to connect with a group of handicapped adults. When they got to this man and saw him assembling the bicycle brake, one of them said spontaneously, "I can't believe that you can do that—It's so complicated!" And the man looked up at him and smiled, the visitor looked back and smiled, and a real connection was made. I just love that idea of competence deviance!

Another teaching technique that was instrumental for us was creating situations for our citizens where the proper response is demanded. Let me elaborate on this very important idea. When we're working with a citizen, or a student, or a child, or a colleague—it's far more effective if we can get that situation to do the "talking" for us. This is not easy to do, but is far more effective and longer lasting than just talking.

Susan is a paraplegic citizen who loves to go swimming. She truly loves the bubblers—those little discs that shoot air bubbles up through the shallow water. She likes to lay down right on top of them and feel the bubbles on her skin. We were trying to encourage Susan to use her arms and upper torso to strengthen that part of her body.

> **She had wisely created a situation where the proper response was demanded.**

She was not an exercise fan, however, and she did not really like to do this sort of exercise—or any other type of exercise for that matter. Our challenge, then, was to try to create a situation that demanded she use her upper body.

Her teacher took Susan into the pool, took her out of her wheelchair, laid her down next to the bubblers (but not on top of them), and said, "Oh, my goodness! I forgot to make an appointment for you! I have to go use the phone!" She told Susan, "I'll be right back to put you over the bubblers." She left Susan there, went into the pool office about ten feet away, and stood by a giant window where she could watch Susan. Susan waited and waited. She finally got tired of waiting, and she began to pull herself over the bubblers with her upper body. That took quite some doing. But Susan did it. Of course, the teacher was there and watching, so that if anything happened she'd be able to run to the rescue quickly. But she had wisely created a situation where the proper response was demanded. When she came back to Susan she did a "Hip, Hip, Hooray" for the accomplishment and gathered all of her colleagues who also applauded. Susan was tickled pink.

Our grandson Wilson has been a Brookwood citizen since 2009, and this same approach was also helpful in encouraging him to ride his three-wheeler. Wilson needs exercise, and fitness is a major part of our program, but Greg couldn't figure out a way to get him to ride the bike. Wilson always had something else he'd rather do, or he would just plain say, "No, I don't want to ride." Greg knew that Wilson loves Santa Claus, so he asked a parent volunteer to take a piece of a sleigh from one of our Christmas plays and attach it to a small wagon behind Wilson's bike.

Greg explained the situation: Wilson needs to drive the sleigh for Santa Claus—it is *critically* important. So now he rides that bike all over the place. He's putting miles and miles on the bike with the sleigh at the back.

A discovery in one area can lead to unexpected and wonderful consequences in another.

At Brookwood, it's amazing how many things are connected, and how often a discovery in one area can lead to unexpected and wonderful consequences in another. I can recall one instance in which a solution for a single citizen's challenge became a useful tool we would eventually use throughout our community.

Kevin is an outstanding young man, but he used to wander—and sometimes he would wander in the night. We talked to him about it, and he tried his best not to do it again, but then he'd forget and wander off. We were constantly watching him, and we also put an alarm on the door so that when it was opened from the inside, the alarm would alert his home teachers, and they would come and re-direct him. Of course, it alerted everyone else in the house, also!

Then we realized another way we could utilize Dr. Mesibov's TEACCH method. It is an outstanding, visually-cued communication tool, so we got a picture of a red, hexagonal stop sign and put it on the door. Kevin knew what stop signs meant, and when he saw the sign, he would stop, turn around, and go back to his room. It worked beautifully.

The use of pictures to communicate has been in use in education for years. Dr. Mesibov formalized it, developing and standardizing visual symbols that came to be used very effectively for some children with autism. At Brookwood, as we've said, we have adapted it to the adult, and we use picture stories rather than words when we have a challenge in communication. We routinely give instructions, make announcements, prepare a schedule, remind about hygiene, and extend sympathy, etc., using this method. We use it in the residential program, in all of our enterprises, and activities. We have Kevin's wandering to thank for showing us how adaptable it could be.

I remember well one of our very high-level citizens who was extremely difficult to deal with when she first came, and the TEACCH method was instrumental in helping her, too. Jan had been in institution after institution and hospital after hospital, to no avail, and her behavior was really undermining the other citizens at Brookwood. She would not follow instructions, she became angry at small challenges, and she didn't seem to care about anything or anybody. We felt she comprehended us when we talked, but she resolutely refused to comply. She had verbally convinced us that she did understand what we said but truly she did not.

When the visually-cued instruction program was introduced, we made a notebook for her. We included pictures of her mother and her dad, of their car, and of what she liked to eat, as well as ways for her to tell us if she felt bad, who she liked to work with, instructions for the task at hand, and everything else we could think of—in spite of her objections to "that baby book." One day I was taking a group on a tour, and explaining to them about how important it is when we think we're communicating with someone to be sure that they actually understand us. We may *believe* there is comprehension between the two parties, but many, many times there is *not*. Even in "normal" society, you may think you're on the same wavelength with someone, only to find out that you're missing—just by a fraction of an inch, perhaps—but you're missing.

At first when we gave the "picture notebook" to this young lady and asked for confirmation that she understood what we wanted, she would respond rather vehemently, "Yes-s-s, I do. Yes-s-s, I do understand."

"Well," we would say, "we just wanted to make sure."

Then she would respond (more gruffly than before), "You have made it very clear to me, and I DO UNDERSTAND. Do you understand that I understand?"

Well, this went on and on and on, and we knew that she was either deliberately being oppositional, or she simply couldn't help it. We weren't sure which. So we continued to use this visually-cued instruction at every opportunity. Then on the day I was taking a tour group through Brookwood and explaining visually-cued instruction, I saw her and asked, "Jan, could we borrow your book just a minute so that I could show these folks how important this program of visually-cued communication is?

> No matter how many new techniques we have tried, the lessons of our greatest mentors…remain integral to our program today.

"Oh, no! Oh, no, Mrs. Streit!" she protested. "No! I'm like Linus. That book's my security blanket. I can't let go of it. I even sleep with it."

That is how much the visually-cued instruction—storytelling—matters to our citizens. Now, computer programs are available with all the visual symbols teachers use. It is absolutely amazing. And Jan is now one of the stalwarts at Brookwood, due in part to the ability to communicate with comprehension. You can see why we are such big fans of Dr. Mesibov!

Over the years, we have learned that by utilizing and modifying the various techniques of other experts, some of them will work for our people, and some will not. Because we are determined to keep evolving and improving, we never forget my parents' important lesson: if something is not working, don't give up, just try another way! No matter how many new techniques we have tried, the lessons of our greatest mentors, like Dr. Kephart, Dr. Gold, and Dr. Mesibov, remain integral to our program today.

NETWORK DAYS

Way back when, soon after we moved into a building of our own at The Briarwood School, we began to get requests from people to come to observe how we were working with children who had special challenges. I think that these requests emanated by word of mouth from families and doctors. In the beginning we would have about one or two sets of visitors a month come and spend from a few hours to a full day under the guidance of one of our key staff members. From this developed an informal internship program. Some of these interns would come one day a week, some came everyday for three weeks, and others six weeks. We were delighted and flattered that others saw the benefit of our program and wanted to learn, and we were eager to share and learn from them also. This practice continued when we added The Brookwood Community. In fact, two groups of interns came to Brookwood from Germany for three months. Soon, the number of requests grew to about three or four groups a month. The opportunity for experiential learning was a success, but the number of visitors was taking a toll on our key staff. Ultimately, this sharing of experiences with teachers, families, and others from the medical profession had to be limited because of staff and time restraints. But the numbers of people who wanted to learn from us had increased markedly, so we realized that we simply must try another way—thus evolved Network Days.

Our Advancement Department took over and developed a well-organized program that took place several times a year for two or three days at a time. The success of these conferences had spread and we had organizations and individuals coming from all over the U.S. and from countries around the world. Instead of folks coming to visit at many and varied times during the year, we set up specific times for them to come. We could offer an even better program and also allow our staff to concentrate on presenting their material more successfully while still working efficiently with their number one mission—that of providing a better life for our Brookwood citizens. We offered seminars in the various divisions of our community such as: Health and Wellness, Residential, Business, Education, Facilities Management, Human Relations, Special Events, Fundraising, Administration, Admission, Marketing, Enterprises, Product Design and Production, Horticulture, etc. As the Network Days program continues to evolve, we see it moving into the next realm of development, currently called the Center for Learning. We are still in the design stage of this institute type concept. We're consulting with those who have done similar programs in order to profit from their experiences and to provide the best programs possible for our constituents. We will continue with the current Network Days format until we move to the new more defined approach. We believe that we will be able to develop this program, pragmatic

Participants at one of Brookwood's
Network Days conferences.

education in tandem with life, into a valid, *certifiable* growth opportunity for educators, families, the medical profession and others so that together we can truly enhance the lives of the multitude of people in one of the fastest growing segments of society today. Collaboration in this type of setting will allow all of us to advance to St. Jerome's avowal: "Good, better, best. Never let it rest. Until your good is better and your better is best."

Outreach participants from Thailand.

REALIZING YOUR CHILD IS DIFFERENT

I know what it is like to have an involved child. For the last fifty years I have encouraged and listened with real empathy to mothers and fathers, sisters, aunts, grandparents and friends of children with differences. I have told them and I can tell you, at times—as with any child—it can be difficult, hopeful, joyous, overwhelming—just about every emotion you can think of. We all worry about our children, but when you have a child who can't function healthfully or safely you also think, "What on earth is going to happen to him or her when I'm gone?"

With Vicki, the first question we asked ourselves was "Will she live? Will she be alive tomorrow?" I stood by that crib hour after hour, praying that she could live. I really wasn't worried about what was going to happen to her later. I didn't know that there was going to *be* a later. I was desperate. When she survived, my desperation took a new form. Desperation is your middle name when you have people who are rather profoundly involved. You love them so dearly and so deeply that you can't help but worry about what's going to happen to them. I remember reading one mother's words. She said, "I know that when I die, I won't even be able to close my eyes, because there will be no one to watch my daughter." I knew how she felt.

I distinctly remember one parent who had a very involved child, and we weren't having much luck in getting him to calm down. This mother couldn't take it any longer. Her husband was gone a lot during the week. He traveled; so most of the responsibility was on her, along with the younger brother. She called me one day and said she wanted to thank me for all we had done for her son. And then she said she wanted to apologize for what she was getting ready to do. I thought, "Oh, no. Help, Lord."

She said, "I have him under the dining room table with me. And I'm holding him down. I'm going to kill him, and then I'm going to kill myself. And I wanted you to know, so somebody could take care of Joe." (Joe was the little brother.)

I didn't want to get off the phone with her, and we didn't have portable phones in those days, so I immediately signaled my secretary. She knew I was really scared. I scribbled a note that said, "Get the psychiatrist on the phone *now!*" That wonderful secretary did a incredible job of getting the psychiatrist on the line in just a minute or two. I put the phone on speaker so the psychiatrist could hear her. I asked her to tell me again all that she had told me previously. She said, "You know how horrible it is. I can't live with this any longer. I've got to relieve him, and relieve myself, and my family."

The doctor took charge, and told me what to do and say. He quickly got his resident over to the house (he had an office nearby), and talked her out of it. That's the most extreme example we have had of desperation, but I could understand her motivation. She didn't know where to turn, she didn't know what to do, and she needed help. And when someone is that desperate, it is no time to sit back and criticize her for what she might do—because I've been utterly desperate, and I know that there is usually no line of reasoning that will help. And if you have ever felt desperate, you understand that, too. Desperation can be a major hurdle on our path. This family weathered that storm and things settled down. They are living a fulfilling life and are moving on.

Desperation can be a major hurdle on our path.

What Vicki and Brookwood have taught me is that *reason* is not always where the answers lie. Sometimes we have to let go of being in charge and let God steer us. How do we do that? Pray, pray, and pray some more. Ask to see things with new eyes. Ask to see what He has provided, what seeds are present in the situation, rather than focusing on what is missing or what we had hoped would happen that didn't.

I'd like to share with you one of my favorite stories about this supernatural way of seeing. It was written by Emily Perl Kingsley, and perhaps you have heard it before, but to me, it is well worth repeating. It goes something like this:

> Planning to have a baby is like planning to go on a wonderful trip, say to Italy. You buy guidebooks, and you make plans for how you will spend your time, you do extensive research, change your money to lira, you pack, and you're ready to go. You get on the plane, but when you land, the flight attendant says, "Welcome to Holland!"
>
> And you say, "Oh, my golly! I've gotten on the wrong plane! I didn't want to go to Holland—I wanted to go to Italy. I wanted to see the Coliseum and the Vatican, the Trevi Fountain and all the wonderful ruins, and the beautiful countryside of Tuscany and Umbria."
>
> But the attendant says, "Well, you may need to change your plans. Holland is a *wonderful* place. It's an amazing, inspirational place. There are just as many sites to see and experiences to have here as there are in Italy. There are windmills and tulips and quaint homes with wooden shoes on the steps, gorgeous canals with gondolas *and,* there are Rembrandts!" But if all you can do is focus on your disappointment about not being in Italy, there's no way for you to appreciate all the wonderful things you can only find in Holland. Allow God to lead you into this new adventure and you will find the reward is greater than you could have imagined. He will lead you along fresh trails of discovery, revealing to you things you did not—and could not—know.

When you are expecting a baby and he or she turns out to be a different child than you had thought you were going to have, you are shocked, disappointed, even devastated. The story of landing in Holland doesn't help you much, because you are certainly going to have to make a lot of adjustments—probably for the rest of your life. An old proverb says: *When the winds of change envelope us, some people build walls and others build windmills.* When you have a handicapped child, you have to ask yourself which are *you* going to build?

Like the Holland story, the experience that you have with a special child is so much about expectation and perspective. When parents first learn they have a handicapped child, for most it's a terrible blow. But for others who have really walked that walk with someone else, it's something very different. My daughter Vivian has two children—Wilson, whom I have mentioned has special needs, and a younger daughter, Sarah. I remember when our granddaughter Sarah was about five, her mother had done a great job in making her proud to have a brother who had a different kind of life, because he could bring new, exciting, and different adventures to *their* lives.

One day Sarah had gone to visit a good friend down the street, whose mother had just come home from the hospital with a new baby. Sarah went down to see the new baby, and she was really fascinated and happy for her friend. She came back to report to her mother and said, "The baby's name is Betsy. But you know what?

> Some people just aren't as lucky as we are.

Mrs. Smith told me that they weren't going to have any more children. And that makes me so sad."

Vivian said, "Well, you know, Sarah, they have three children, and that's kind of a good-sized family."

Sarah said, "No! No! You don't understand! They don't have a handicapped child yet. And now they're not going to have a chance to get one."

Her mother said, "Well, you know, there are a lot of families that don't have handicapped children."

Sarah said, "I know. And it makes me sad." A little bit later, she came back to her mother and said, "I think I've figured it out. I think I know why they don't have a handicapped child."

Her mother said, "Well, why?"

Sarah said, "I just don't think they prayed hard enough."

So that's the feeling Sarah has for handicapped people. It's a new adventure. It's a different adventure. The goals are different, the walk is different, and the parents' role is different. But it's new, it's exciting, it's enlightening, and it's happy most of the time and some of the time very difficult, which may be the closest you get to having a "normal" child adventure. Some people just aren't as lucky as we are.

If a special child has just come into your life, I know you don't believe it now, but the chances are that, within two years in most cases, this child whom your family may be so leery of initially, will begin leading you into new adventures and helping you to discover real joy as a family. For us, this was true, in spite of Vicki's horrific seizures, her sometimes-violent reaction to medication, anxieties, and other challenges. And I'm not speaking just from my own experiences, but the experiences of working with so many hundreds of people over the years.

Keeping close to Him at all times is essential. If you think observing children is important, that doesn't hold a candle to the importance of observing and practicing the presence of God. You do that through living with prayer. So, if you are the parent of a special child, you're going to take on a couple of roles. You're going to be a teacher, of course. That's what every parent is, or should be. And you're going

> **Open your heart to truly, deeply loving this person, just as they are.**

to be a mother or a daddy. Both roles are very important. But the most important job you have is to open your heart to truly, deeply loving this person, just as they are.

When you begin to take care of that child, if your experience is anything like mine and so many that I have witnessed, before you know it you're head over heels in love! What is so exciting is that you are in love in a different way than with your other children. Not a better way, but a *different* way, and with a love that offers a unique adventure not all people are given the opportunity to experience. And, when you experience this, like Sarah, you'll wonder why everyone is not blessed to have a handicapped child.

This unforeseen adventure will keep you very busy, too busy to think much beyond today. But, after about twenty years of having this great adventure with a different type of child, you will probably begin to realize that they need something else—something that even all your determination and love can't provide. You'll begin looking around for a place for your son or daughter to live, in case something should happen to you, or when you come to the end of your life here on earth. You'll want them well cared for, and you will search and search to find a place—perhaps similar to Brookwood. At first you'll be excited about it, and then the time will come for you to bring your child and let him or her start this new life. Then, as they say, *all heck breaks loose.*

In many cases, you are suddenly met with the realization that separating from your child—no matter that child's age—is a traumatic event. You may recognize the fact that the connection between a mother and a father with their special child *is involuntary co-dependency*—each one is deeply dependent upon the other. Some of these parents come in to my office and say, "I can't do it. I cannot part from Joey, or Jenny." And then they'll almost always say to us, "You don't understand." But, since many of our staff have gone through the same or similar challenges we can meaningfully say that we *do* understand.

Having a child with special needs or abilities *is* very special. It's unique—so different from having what we call a "normal" child. Truly, I don't think people without the privilege of having a child with a disability have the slightest idea of what it means to let these children move towards a more independent life. People will say, "Oh, no! I understand. I'm in the 'empty-nest' stage of my life right now. And all of my children have gone on to their own lives." But it's different.

Separating from children with special challenges is so unlike the empty nest syndrome. Although I have never had an amputation, that is about as close as anything I can imagine to the void that I experienced when I was first separated from Vicki. I realize that some families do not feel the same way I did, and that is natural. Some feel a tremendous sense of relief. Some feel joy. Some feel release from a burden, and some simply can't make the move. Speaking for myself, I was joined at the hip with Vicki, and at the shoulders, and at the head, and in every way. For those like me, when that kind of connection and daily purpose is taken away, it is such a major void initially that it's almost impossible to explain. But I will try.

VICKI MOVES TO BROOKWOOD

Vicki has been here so long that most everyone thinks she has been a resident since the beginning, especially because she was such an integral part of why it developed. But like I said, she and I were so connected that we were co-dependent upon each other, and it wasn't all that clear to me back then if I would ever be able to let her live somewhere else—even somewhere that I had spent all my time trying to help God create for her, and people like her.

Then, one day, Dave and I were going on a trip. My mother and dad were getting older, and I knew I couldn't ask them to keep Vicki for the weeks that we'd be gone. I was talking to Rick DeMunbrun about it, and he started laughing hysterically. "I cannot believe you!" he said. "What on earth are you thinking? This is the craziest thing I've ever heard of! Here you have started a community that is running beautifully, everybody loves it, and you don't know where to put your daughter? That is absolutely ridiculous. Now. She will come here, she will do fine, and you will go on your trip and not worry about it, *not one iota.*"

Well, he totally shamed me into saying, "Okay. We'll do it." So we took Vicki to Brookwood, and even though I *knew* how good it was, I was still hesitant about leaving her in the care of others. *Silly mother.* When we got back from our trip, we went racing to get her and "save her from the villains." We picked her up, and took her down to the 7-Eleven to get a Coke and some chips. She was glad to see us—no doubt about that. We turned around and went back, and we were pulling into the Inn where she had been staying so we could get her things to take her home. Well, before the car had come to a complete stop, she opened the car door, jumped out, and ran *home*. Vicki does not talk in words, remember, but she told us loud and clear how she felt. You talk about mixed emotions. I was so glad to see her *want* to run back to Brookwood, and so sad to see her (in my mind) rejecting us. Oh, golly. What a time.

You know, she stayed; we didn't take her to our home. She obviously didn't want to go to what we considered home—she wanted to stay in *her* new home. It was wonderful, and it was awful! There was that void in me that I still can't explain; I can't make anybody understand it, except someone who's gone through it. Now, we're so grateful, and we realize that, inadvertently, we had been standing in the way of allowing her to *soar in her sky.* Letting go of someone or something you love is hard, no matter what you hope the future might hold.

> **For the butterfly to emerge, the cocoon must be broken.**

The story of the cocoon is so true. For the butterfly to emerge, the cocoon must be broken. We had Vicki in a safe and secure little cocoon, and that butterfly could never have emerged had it not been for Brookwood. Now, when I watch her in the mornings from my office, I can see her walking to work with enthusiasm and great anticipation of what that day holds for her. That butterfly is flying high. And this mother is watching with gratefulness.

SEPARATION ANXIETY

Because of my own experience with Vicki, I am not surprised that most families who come to us have many *what if* questions about separating from their loved one. I remember one instance specifically, because it was so illustrative of perspective. Compassion allows us to get a glimpse of someone else's perspective, but not ever in its entirety. Just prior to John's enrollment date, his mother told us that the most important thing in John's life, from his perspective, was "going to see Aunt Louise in Beaumont the third Friday of every month. And is it going to be okay," she asked, "if we continue to do that?"

> **Compassion allows us to get a glimpse of someone else's perspective, but not ever in its entirety.**

PHOTO

GALLERY

PIONEER STAFF

Abraham

Faye

Joyce R.

Greg

Debbie

Yvonne

Rita

Joyce H.

Sylvia

Rick

Ruthie

The farmhouse, Brookwood's
first building.

Our first Brookwood stonecast
shop in the old garage.

Our first greenhouses.

Adrien planting plugs in Horticulture.

Vicki getting pots ready for planting.

Tom teaching Joanie how to put plants in pots.

Gayle packing tomatoes in our hydroponic project.

Carolyn loves planting seedlings.

Taking cuttings for the pots.

Taking poinsettia seedlings to the greenhouses

Margaret says, "They are finally ready!"

Ready for shipping.

Matt working on our first saleable product.

Dean preparing a mold.

Wayne pouring a stonecast mold.

John opening a mold.

Eileen painting a stonecast
Comfort Bowl.

Diane painting crosses.

Joe, Yvonne, Barbara Bush and Susan Baker
visiting with Jenny.

Mark working on a concrete garden statue.

Cheryl, Vicki, and Nancy stenciling a ceramic plate.

Paul cleaning a ceramic piece.

A busy day at our wonderful café.

Colleen and Farris, two of our superstar volunteers.

Mesibov bottling crew.

Richard delivering food utilizing the
TEACCH method.

Our initial Brookwood sign.

Our first makeshift store in the old farmhouse.

The first real store.

The present Sherren Smith Gift and Garden Center.

Linda Lou says decorating the store is "exhausting."

YOUR PURCHASES SUPPORT BROOKWOOD CITIZENS

Retail Greenhouse.

"Retirement with a purpose" volunteers Harold and Ferne.

Outside at the Garden Center.

An outstanding Fine Art Gallery in the Retail Store.

Shudde helping Shudde with a hat.

Jeff knows that hobbies are important.

Carolyn, Betsy, and
Dr. Harrison at the dental clinic.

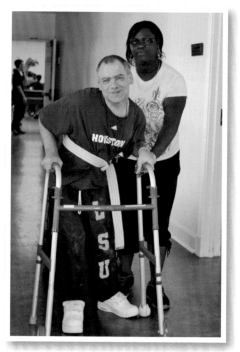

Fitness training with Dwight and Rachel.

Bob loves animals.

Tuttle Group Home.

The Streit-Tuttle Clan at the Tuttle Home dedication.

Mark doing household chores.

Bruce, Chad, and Jason relaxing at their home.

Toby coaching Kim in soccer.

Gerald racing against the clock.

Aqua Fitness.

Practicing for the "Olympics."

Working on balance.

Our goal is 300 miles this year.

Handbell Choir at the Christmas pageant.

Handbell Choir at the Houston Grand Opera Gala.

Chris, Cerebral Palsy, and music mix well.

Executive Director Vivian serving Dennis and
Joanie at the New Year's Gala.

Kenny, Margaret, Joe and Chase playing the bongos.

Citizen Joe and co-author Jana are buddies.

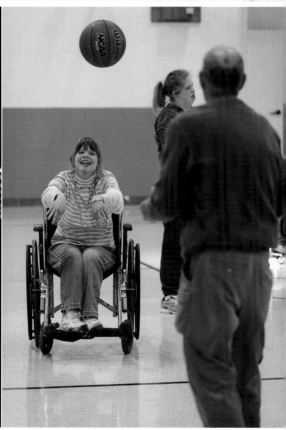

Alex…loves making music.

Good throw Melissa.

Aerial view of the Brookwood central campus.

Sharing successes and failures with
participants from Mexico City through our
Network Days Conferences.

Our citizens are what make
Brookwood special.

Stacy preparing an angel ornament for glazing.

Vicki, one of our angels.

The Worship Center interior.

The Worship Center.

God's chair where everyone is welcome.

We said, "Of course, but let's wait a few weeks for John to become accustomed to Brookwood, and then let him go." Several weeks later, his mother called and asked if it was all right to take John to see Aunt Louise in Beaumont. We said we thought that would be nice, but asked her to please call and check with John, which she did.

To her surprise, in answer to the question, "Do you want to go see Aunt Louise in Beaumont?" John said, almost through tears, "Oh, Mother! I can't go! You see, I am now a member of the human race."

His mother was in shock—not in his not wanting to go, so much as in the intensity of his response, and her new awareness of his feelings about himself. Her thoughts took her from the joy of his new self-esteem to the depths of guilt, where she thought, "I have not done a good job with John. I've not allowed him the opportunities he needed to grow." Guilt affects most of us, and I am a master at cultivating it within myself. I explained to this wonderful mother that this was a part of growth and that she had simply opened a door to a new opportunity. John had been in a critically important, protective cocoon, and the right time had come for the butterfly to emerge. Without the family preparing the way, this probably would not have happened. None of us knows the perfect way to handle these situations or the perfect timing, because none of us is perfect.

I'll tell you something else about perfection that I learned from our grandson Wilson. We were at church one day, and our minister was talking about how people strive for perfection, and they find it impossible to achieve. He went on to say, "There is not anybody that's perfect. Now if there's anybody in this congregation who thinks they're perfect, please raise your hand." Well, Wilson only heard "Raise your hand." So up his hand went. Dave and I were pulling his hand down, but the minister noticed it. He smiled and said, "Well, if there's anybody close to it in this whole congregation, it's you, Wilson."

Wilson and Stacy are a planting team.

IV.

B L O S S O M S

For so many years of the Brookwood journey, when we arrived at a significant milestone, we were shown that there was something more we needed to do. Early on, my focus was to find a way to help Vicki. Then we needed a school to help her and others like her to get the practical education they needed. Then, we needed a place where these kiddoes, all grown up now, could continue working, learning, and living.

And once we acquired our land and the Brookwood campus you see today was developing, it might seem like we had finally reached our goal and could simply settle in, but that is never the case. Life moves on, and God calls us to keep responding to the needs and challenges of each new day. Over time, it became apparent to us that functionally-disabled adults—just like any other adult—will one day come to the end of their lives and move on to a better place. When I was young, the news that a "mongoloid" (the accepted term for a person with Down Syndrome in those days) had lived to be twelve years old was newsworthy enough to make the front page of the *Houston Chronicle*. Today, due to wonderful advances in medical science, people with Down syndrome live considerably longer, and people with disabilities make up one of the fastest-growing segments of our society today. Determining these individuals' place in that society is an exciting challenge, but to do so we must address how to care for them as they age.

Hooray! We just finished planting 48,000 poinsettias.

HONORING THE END OF LIFE

We buried a lady with Down Syndrome this past year who was seventy-eight. She and other citizens have opened our eyes to ways that Brookwood can help others enter each successive stage of life with grace and dignity. These citizens often provide us with a clear vision of what God's path is when it is not obscured by our attempts to control.

Judy is one such citizen who was not with us long, but whose spirit and special challenges made a powerful impact on our community. Judy was the victim of *osteogenesis imperfecta*, a disease that causes the entire skeletal structure to weaken and become extremely susceptible to breaking. Both of her parents had died, and she had no other living relatives. Fortunately, two loving neighbor-ladies God had somehow recruited, attended to her needs, and these women—after much prayer and study—took it upon themselves to provide the care she needed. Judy was in a wheelchair, but it wasn't a normal wheelchair. It reclined to an almost horizontal position because, if she sat up, the weight of her body would crack the bones in her spine. She was very fragile and very, very small—maybe only four feet tall—and she weighed next to nothing. Judy had been protected, hovered over, and beautifully cared for all of her life.

Because her parents had been afraid to take her anywhere for fear her bones might break, Judy really had never been out of the house. But her two neighbors thought it would be wonderful for her to see the outside world, and they outfitted their car so that she could recline, yet still be high enough to look out the window when they went for rides. Eventually they heard about Brookwood and came out for a visit. We all decided that we should let Judy come to our community for a trial period. We took her around in her "wheelcot," and she participated in a few of the activities that we had. Judy was in her mid-twenties when she came to us, and obviously required a lot of TLC. Her mental and emotional conditions were amazing, however, and somehow she was able to minister to *all* with whom she came in contact.

One day, she stopped me after she had been at Brookwood for just a short time and said with such emotion and sincerity, "Oh, Mrs. Streit. I did not know that life could be like this. Thank you." It brought tears to my eyes—she was just amazing. In fact as I write this story for you, it brings back tears of gratitude that I was able to meet Judy, who exhibited such joy and peace within and taught us all.

She had not been at Brookwood long before Judy accidentally turned herself in her wheelcot, breaking her arm and some fragile vertebrae in her back. As much as we loved her, we had to face the fact that we were simply not equipped to give Judy the kind of care she required. Her doctors agreed, and advised her angel caregivers to put her in a skilled nursing facility where the staff was trained to care for folks with acute medical needs. She didn't live very long after she left us, but I know she's free from all encumbrances now.

Judy's short time at Brookwood helped us to understand so much. Yes, we could do a lot for a good many folks, but we couldn't meet the needs of everyone. We saw that, inevitably, some people under our care would eventually need a different *kind* of support than we were able to offer. A far better place for adults with functional disabilities had come into being, but we were not equipped to handle some challenges. Even so, end-of-life issues were clearly something that we would have to address.

ADDRESSING THE NEEDS OF THE AGING

The aging process affects all of us differently, yet it is not unusual to see the elderly lumped into a group, labeled and disregarded, just as the disabled often are. The one-size-fits-all mentality is not appropriate in either case. Certainly at Brookwood we have come to value the complete uniqueness of every individual, and we refuse to marginalize anyone because of his or her age, disability, or any other characteristic. We believe that all people—including the aged—have something inside that can blossom into a valuable contribution.

At Brookwood we want to care for *all* citizens as though they were members of our very own family. We all have the *need to be needed*, and that purpose is just as important in our waning years as it is in our younger years. So often, people retire with a treasure of knowledge and wisdom acquired through years of experience, and it isn't being used. It's being wasted. Perhaps if we could incorporate retirees valuable life experiences for the good of the community as we do at Brookwood with our disabled citizens' gifts, we could enhance everyday life for these older individuals—socially, emotionally, physically, and spiritually—and also provide better care for our ever-increasing numbers of citizens who are living far longer than ever before.

> We believe that all people— including the aged—have something inside that can blossom into a valuable contribution.

This very important concept is coming to life here at Brookwood even now. We are establishing another section, or subdivision, designed to incorporate the ever-growing segment of society called the retirees. It is a place where the regular retiree can come to live and become an asset to this mission by simply being present in the village or by participating more actively in the everyday needs of the program or the individual citizens. These new members of our community could work with the citizens in the artisan shops, help with transportation, help in maintenance or any of the jillion other areas that make up the Brookwood campus, or they could just be a friend—perhaps the most important way to help. We are calling this *Retirement with a Purpose*, and we believe it is a win-win opportunity.

Our own citizens, who have had unique needs all their lives, also have a wide range of needs as they age. We are always adapting in order to make sure that we provide them the appropriate environment. It is a fairly well established fact that the Down Syndrome adult will eventually fall victim to Alzheimer's, so another addition that we made at Brookwood was remodeling and upgrading the Kilroy Home as a residence for our citizens who need additional care because of failing memory. This has worked out beautifully. It is still a residential home with regular rooms, but with more support than is offered in our other homes.

When we look at these important end-of-life issues, we see a beautiful analogy to a river. There is a river—let's call it the River of Life—flowing through the land. We enter it on one shore where we need an awful lot of help; as infants and young children we're very, very dependent. Then, as we move deeper into the river, toward its center, we become more independent. We don't feel as "needy" as we did in the beginning; in fact, at this point in the river, some people feel as if they're *completely* independent (which, by the way, can never really be true. We're always dependent on something or someone or some set of circumstances.) Then, as we move from the center toward the opposite shore, we realize that, once again, we need the help of others to reach the other side. We're still in the river–in the flow of life—but we're on the periphery. The important thing is that until we reach the opposite shore we have the opportunity to remain *in the river* and not be isolated from the main flow of the working world.

We consider it a positive thing that many of our citizens here at Brookwood have died where they have lived and been loved. We have kept them "in the river" as it flows, with their friends, their work, and their security. Some have been with their coworkers at work the day they died. Our friend Laura, one of our elderly citizens, was unaware of her surroundings in her last hours, but she had spent time in the living room with her friends just that evening. Before morning, she had moved to the "next chapter" of her life. We acknowledge and honor death in our community, and it's been very rewarding to see how our citizens accept death as an important part of life.

After Laura died, one of our citizens asked if he could tell his home teacher a story about his friend Johnny. The teacher

> **It's been very rewarding to see how our citizens accept death as an important part of life.**

said that he would love to hear Johnny's story, so with moderate difficulty (his speech was impaired), the citizen told this story: "My friend Johnny was dying of a bad sickness and I asked him if he was scared to die. And you know what? Johnny said no, he wasn't afraid. The reason he wasn't afraid was because he had asked his mother what it was going to be like when he died. His mother told him that she didn't know for sure, but that they could ask God for help with the answer. They did, and a few minutes later, she said that she thought it might be similar to when Johnny used to play soccer and would come home very, very, very tired, and sometimes go to sleep on the couch. Later, his daddy would gently pick him up and take him to his bed upstairs and tuck him in. Then his mother said, "I think it may be like that, but this time it will be Jesus who picks you up and takes you to *His* Father, and that will be good. Then later on, Jesus will come and get us, and we will all be together. So you see, there is nothing to be afraid of."

Through his tears, the home teacher said, "I think that is the best story I have ever heard. Thank you for telling me about Johnny." Talking with each other about aging and illness and death is one way we seek to make it a natural part of life. Our citizens seem to understand, and they exhibit great kindness toward one another in times of sadness and loss, just as they do in times of joy and celebration. Accepting each other as God has made us is one of the most important steps we can make towards understanding the unconditional love that He shows us. We are all imperfect mirrors, but when we allow our hearts to be open the way our citizen's are, that love becomes so much more visible in our lives.

> Talking with each other about aging and illness and death is one way we seek to make it a natural part of life.

As I hope the stories that I have told you so far have shown, Brookwood is more than a place in the country, or even more than a special group of individuals. It's a way of life expressed in a powerful set of values—and those values color everything we do. Let me tell you a few more of my favorite Brookwood stories to illustrate how these values are integrated into the everyday life of the community.

UNCONDITIONAL LOVE

U nconditional love is a foundational value at Brookwood, and Mitzi's story is probably one of the most dramatic examples that I could tell of such love. Mitzi's parents learned of Brookwood through a very well written article in the *Houston Chronicle*. After the article ran, we had a large number of families coming to see us and wanting to put their adult child in Brookwood, and Mitzi's family was one of these.

When her parents came in, they explained that they had four children; one, Mitzi, was so disruptive and aggressive that they had felt it was best to put her in a facility. They had always wanted a place more like home for her, and from the very first day Mitzi entered that facility, they began planning to move her to a place where she would be loved and have as good a life as possible.

Her family had saved diligently in order to make this goal possible, and her parents urged us to "please consider taking her." They told stories about Mitzi that impressed us greatly; some of them were not very positive, but the stories were honest, and her parents sincerely believed that if she were cared for in a different way, Mitzi's more troublesome behaviors might diminish.

Rick DeMunbrun and I listened sympathetically, but we had real concerns. Because Mitzi was both self-abusive and aggressive, hurting people around her, we felt she would probably *not* be a good fit for Brookwood. But then remembering the many rejections that our Vicki had experienced, I felt another God nudge, and we told Mitzi's parents that we would observe her once again at the other facility before deciding. We found her closed-off and alone. Rick saw her, and his heart went out to her. He came back, and said, "I don't know why I feel this way, because it doesn't make sense, but I think that we ought to give it a try. But I'll be honest—it does *not* look promising."

So Mitzi moved to Brookwood, and sure enough, she was all that the reports had said. She acted very aggressively. Fortunately, she did not hit any of our citizens; however she lashed out at the staff, she kicked the chairs, and she walked around in what looked like a semi-fetal position. Mitzi had no language; she screamed at the top of her lungs. We kept her apart from the other residents in the beginning, and we kept her parents informed constantly. We saw and felt their desperation. There were four or five staff members who were her primary caregivers and, amazingly, in spite of the multitude of challenges, they wanted to continue to work with Mitzi.

We decided, collectively, that we were not going to respond to her behavior in a punitive way; but, instead, as Rick suggested, we would *love it out of her.* We would let her know we really did care. A few months went by, and we began to see a glimpse—just a tiny glimpse—of her holding her head up just a little, and standing a bit straighter. More time went by, and she was walking almost upright, and even looking us in the eye for a brief second, before looking back down. The kicking had stopped (at least she didn't run after people to kick at them); and she had learned to weed a flowerbed (her choice of occupations) properly and did that job better than anyone else. Her teachers said that she had become one of the best workers in all of horticulture. Mitzi began following us with her eyes, participated in a few fitness activities, and did not intrude on others' space. Three or four years went by, and I think one of the sweetest things that I've ever had happen to me was when Mitzi looked me in the eyes and blew me a kiss. I can't tell you what that meant. It's touching to this very minute.

Mitzi was truly in love, a father/daughter type of devotion, with one of our home teachers, Carl. I've never witnessed anything quite like it. When he walked by, she followed him with her eyes with a look of pure *adoration.* That loving adoration was just so obvious, and so uplifting. Gosh, it was wonderful. It came from a deep sense of peace and security and love. As so often happens when our citizens give us a window on God's love, this reminded me of how we're led to believe that God feels that same love for us, an assurance that we receive through the presence of the Holy Spirit. Mitzi's spirit began to soar and took the rest of us right along with it.

**Mitzi's spirit began to soar and took the rest
of us right along with it.**

Mitzi lived with us for a number of years, and now she's moved on to heaven. We have a favorite drawing of her that some of her friends at

Brookwood made. It's kind of a story-picture of Mitzi surrounded by lots of hearts, and then a group of our citizens with a big heart, then a picture of Mitzi and Carl who both meant so much to so many, and finally a picture of Jesus pointing to God (who is represented by a blank space, since we don't know what he looks like). At the end, it says "Bye-bye" with a picture of someone blowing a kiss and the words "We'll see you later, Mitzi." This is an example of the kind of "social stories" that mean so much to our entire community–families, staff, and citizens alike.

To me, Mitzi's story sums up so many aspects of Brookwood. Her family had been torn up about what to do with her, and even though she was coming to live with others with functional disabilities, we still had to help her find a way to become a positive part of the community. Her behaviors were almost more than we could imagine handling. But with God's help (and His initial nudge), we were able to show her un-

> **We were able to show her unconditional love rather than rejection, and it changed things for everyone involved.**

conditional love rather than rejection, and it changed things for everyone involved. No one chooses to have a child with disabilities; and no one chooses to be disabled. What we have learned from this community again and again is that everyone has a seed to sow—and that love is a powerful, powerful motivator.

POSITIVE FOCUS

How do we determine what that seed each person has might be? When a new citizen comes to Brookwood, we make it a point to focus on their competencies, and as we do, the citizen begins to take on an identity based on what it is they *can* do. No one at Brookwood is known initially for his or her disability. We certainly don't gloss over that reality, but we focus *first* on their competencies. As we do, just as Dr. Gold's work proved, their deviances recede into the background.

Whether that new citizen is brought into the residential program or the day program, no one sends out an email that says, "This person has seventeen things she's dealing with." The very first introduction of a new citizen to the Brookwood family includes five or six positive things about this person. Their family, interests, hobbies, what they're "famous" for in their hometown, what foods they like, whether or not they like animals, etc. The very first encounter we have with a new citizen is all about their competencies. We want our community to get to know the newest member as another citizen who can help all of us contribute to the world.

> **Our citizens and staff thrive on surmountable challenges.**

Our citizens thrive in community life. There is constant support, opportunities for social, emotional, vocational, and spiritual growth, fun and adventure, and plenty of *surmountable* challenges. Our citizens and staff thrive on surmountable challenges. As they progress in their work, new ideas and competencies are brought forth. They receive praise and encouragement from the thousands of visitors who come through every year and are impressed with the outstanding products they make. It's a constant reward set-up.

But from the staff and administrative standpoint, there are also challenges dealing with residential life at Brookwood. Whom do you match with whom in a home? Will she mesh with the people who are already there? Does he need a downstairs or an upstairs room? Will he flourish in that setting? What needs does she have that our home teachers must meet? If we have too many citizens who have "unmet needs" (that's how we see behavioral challenges), it can be draining on both the teacher and the group. Do we believe that we can turn any negatives that may exist into positives? In this business of matching suitemates and housemates, we must focus on making sure they complement rather than detract from each other. We also consider what kind of emotional coping skills will be needed for them to share living space.

For instance, one of our citizens, Stephen, was a non-stop talker. You may be saying to yourself, "Oh, yes, I know several non-stop talkers," but

I'm talking about a *driven* behavior. For this young man, talking was truly a compulsion. Nobody really understands this unless they've experienced it with someone like Stephen. His chatter was constant, and repetitive, and he simply could not be re-directed. The only time Stephen stopped talking was when he was asleep. To say that he was not a sought after suitemate is an understatement. We couldn't *keep* a suitemate with him—until Patrick came along. This combination worked out perfectly; Stephen's non-stop barrage of words didn't bother his new companion one bit. You see, Patrick was stone deaf.

LIFE-LONG LEARNING (AND PATIENCE)

Another wonderful teacher I had at Briarwood was eleven years old. His name was Monty. He had cerebral palsy and had developed patience that you could not believe. He had to develop patience because everything he did physically was a laborious struggle. He was unable to use his legs, so he had to rely on crutches; he referred to himself as "Tripod." His two legs were rather entwined, so in actuality he thought of them as one leg. Add two crutches to the picture and he became like a tripod. His hands were gnarled, which made using the crutches even more difficult. He had to work hard at everything he did and he did it without a complaint—he was amazing.

One day, I was writing a proposal, which is not one of my favorite things to do. I asked my secretary to please not let anyone in to my office, and no phone calls, and not to disturb me for any reason. I needed all the concentrating time I could get, and interruptions were a giant obstacle. I sat down to write, and before you knew it there was a knock at my hallway door. Needless to say, I was quite upset. When I looked up and saw that it was Monty, I went to the door with a forced smile to see what he wanted. He was grinning up a storm and said in his humble and thoughtful manner: "Mrs. Streit, if you aren't too busy, I would like to show you something." Well, what could I say but "Good, I would love to see it?" He invited me to come over to the stairs with him. I followed, and he stood at the base of the stairs. With superhuman effort, Monty *went up six stairs*. The strength, the determination, and the persistence that it took was so evident that I shouted for joy. I cheered and hugged him, and we all rejoiced in his triumph. He told me that he had been working on that secretly for three months and eleven days, and in our mind that feat was worth an Olympic gold medal. He told me that he wanted to show *me*, because he knew that I was good at waiting and wouldn't mind waiting till he had gotten up all six stairs. Another lesson. Patience comes in many forms. Monty taught me about one of those forms, because until that day I had really *not* been very good at waiting.

Patience comes in many forms.

I went back into my office and said to myself, "If I put one fiftieth of the energy into writing that proposal that he put in his effort, that proposal would be written in thirty minutes." With help from Monty's lesson, the proposal was written. And, by the way, the request was granted. Thank you, Monty!

CELEBRATION

At Brookwood, we not only celebrate feats like Monty's, we celebrate special occasions and milestones, and most of all we celebrate *each other*. We observe holidays like Christmas, New Year's, Thanksgiving, Fourth of July, and of course Halloween and anniversaries. We held a huge celebration on our community's tenth anniversary with over 500 people attending.

We celebrate special occasions and milestones, and most of all we celebrate each other.

We had a carnival, complete with everything from an old-fashioned cakewalk to a trampoline with a safety harness, and a "dunk the staff" tank just for fun. We even had a parade featuring antique cars to

Carol directing Brookwood's Mardi Gras krewe
with King and Queen Joe and Dianna.

kick off the event. Our citizens made floats, and most of them got through
the parade in one piece, but several didn't. (The floats I mean. The citizens
did fine.) Two citizens Bill and Virginia led the parade, holding the American
flag and the Texas flag. The marching music blared, and everyone thought
that they were the most important people in the world. We all loved it.

That was a very special day—but we also celebrate the everyday
accomplishments of our citizens. Because we value helping others, we
encourage Brookwoodians to actively seek out ways to help their neighbors, their friends, their homes, and their community. We often ask, "Did
you see somebody do something good today?" Or, "What are you giving
thanks for today? What can you do for someone else that would please
them, and please God?" We try to celebrate work well done: "How many

plants did we plant today?" And, to see the results: "How many plants grew from what we planted last month? Did we do it the right way?"

One of our special points of focus at Brookwood is doing for others both *in* our community and *outside* it. Not long ago, Brookwood citizens took up a collection at our worship service for "Wheels Across Africa," a group that provides wheelchairs for disabled Africans who have never had a way to get around, except to crawl. This outreach was instigated by one of our wheelchair-bound citizens. He had seen pictures of some Africans who were crawling in the dirt in order to get where they were going. They only had one wheelchair for the tribe. It was a wooden chair that had a makeshift axel under the seat. It had wheels on it, but they didn't stay on very long. He was so touched by the pictures, that he sent a dollar to the church that was trying to help this tribe. When the African group came to Houston, they made a visit to Brookwood. Greg took this project under his wing (his angel wing), and we have tried to help ever since. We recognize that all of us have weaknesses; all of us have strengths. Reaching out to help someone else gives us an even greater understanding of others than just being recipients of kindness ever could. Generosity is something we love to celebrate.

Laughter is often a part of Brookwood celebrations—and laughing together underscores the things we have in common. Laughter smooths a lot of roads. Underneath their challenges, Brookwoodians are first people like you and me, and only secondarily less abled in some ways, as we are also. They have emotional lives that are just like those of regularly-abled people, with strong likes, dislikes, favorite foods, special friends, and preferences of all kinds. Our citizen Bill received a compliment one day on how nice he looked in the bright red jacket that he always wears at open house. He replied, "Yes, I like this, because all the ladies like me when I wear it so it is important that I wear it." We all know gentlemen who dress to impress the ladies!

Laughter smooths a lot of roads.

Another citizen, James, was getting ready for our New Year's Gala. At this event, our citizens "dress to the nines"—there are formal dresses for the women, and rented tuxedos donated by a local company for the men. I was standing at the foot of the stairs at our largest home, and James was coming down the stairs attired in his tuxedo. When he got to me he said, "Mrs. Streit, could I 'ax' you a question?" I said, "Of course." He looked down at his tuxedo and cummerbund and then back at me and said, "Just who am I marryin'? Because I had always planned to remain a 'batchela'!" He was relieved to learn that his plans on that account did not need to change.

(Left to right) Yvonne, Vicki, and Dave at the New Year's Gala.

PERSPECTIVE

Perspective is another essential value at Brookwood. Sometimes just looking at something in a different way can change frustration to joy and failure to victory. In the early years, we had a basketball team that overcame some pretty formidable odds. At first our team was just a group of individuals who stood near each other underneath a basketball hoop. We hadn't learned yet how to depend on each other or work together. Our gym in those days, as I have mentioned, was a gravel driveway, the backboard was tilted, and the goal

> Sometimes just looking at something in a different way can change frustration to joy and failure to victory.

had a rim, of course, but no net. It didn't matter though–we enjoyed it as it was and became pretty good at the game.

One year our basketball team made it through the Special Olympics tournament to the regional finals, which were being held in San Antonio. It was so exciting—we were one of the final two teams. We were ahead 31 to 30 with only thirty seconds to go and we had the ball! We were, dribbling and passing the ball to one another, then—lo and behold—Jared, one of our star players, scored a basket for the other team. We lost 32-31. Somehow, in all the commotion, our players didn't seem to mind. Jared had scored; they kept congratulating him, and we came home victorious. It really *is* all in your perspective.

Brookwoodians often do see things differently, and beautifully. One of our employees recalled a conversation she overheard between two citizens while driving the Brookwood bus back to Houston. "I'm so glad we get to take the HOV lane," the first citizen said. "It's so much faster!" When the second citizen then asked what the HOV lane was, the first citizen said, "It stands for 'High *Occupation* Vehicle. We can take it because we have highly important jobs." I couldn't agree more.

COMPASSION

Then there is compassion. This is a value I see demonstrated daily at Brookwood. You might think our citizens would be focused on themselves and their own needs—but they "see" in a way that others do not. We were keeping our grandson Wilson when the mother of one of our staff members, Isla Jean, died. We needed to go by the funeral home for the visitation, and we explained to Wilson (who speaks and even whispers *very* loudly) that he needed to go in the funeral home with us, but he was not to talk, not even in a whisper. He was to sit quietly on the couch until we were ready to leave. "We will only be a few minutes," we told him, "and then we'll go out and get some frozen yogurt."

We went in, Wilson sat down on the couch, and he was quiet as a church mouse. We talked to Isla Jean for a few minutes, and gave her our condolences. Then Wilson came up, and in his stage whisper voice, said, "Memaw! Can I say something to Isla Jean?" Well, of course everybody heard him, so how could I say no?

"Well, yes," I told him, "You can say something to Isla Jean."

So Wilson turned to her and said in a very simple, factual (and loud) way, "Isla Jean, we not sorry for your mama. She's with God in heaven, and she's happy. But we sorry for you, Isla Jean. We love you."

And the people standing around said, "Well, that's about the best sermon I've heard in a long time."

We learn lessons like this from our citizens in every program area, and we have been witnessing them from the earliest days. One day, as I was ringing the bell to call our staff and citizens tó lunch from the tree farm where they were working, I saw my daughter Vicki, who seemingly is not very aware of her surroundings. On her way to lunch she walked past Karen, who was wheeling herself with great difficulty along a gravel path.

Vicki helping Karen over a rough road.

Everyone else was already in the building. Vicki passed Karen and then stopped. She looked around and saw that there was no one else in sight, and then she went back and started pushing Karen in her wheelchair. She wasn't able to push her very well or very far, but her action showed a very basic desire to help another person. It was a beautiful and inspiring gesture, and I was so proud of her. The compassion in that simple act is exactly what we try to teach and demonstrate: look around and try to find people in need, and then ask

> **Look around and try to find people in need, and then ask yourself, "Is there a way I can help?"**

yourself, "Is there a way I can help?" And if so, are you willing to do it? Because of Vicki's mental deficiencies, we assumed that she was totally unaware of Karen's plight, but something deep within moved her to help her teammate. *Love is an active verb.*

INTERDEPENDENCE

Karen and Christine helping each other.

Christine and Karen are two special citizens whom I call the "Bobsey twins." They are not actually twins, but they are always together. Christine has cerebral palsy and does not have use of her legs; Karen is blind, but she can walk with assistance. They have a side-by-side tandem bike. Karen, whose legs work, does the peddling, while Christine, whose eyes work, does the steering. Together, they've got a really good thing going, helping one another. They are a living example of interdependence—another important value at The Brookwood Community.

GENEROSITY

Brookwood is the product of so much generosity—it's humbling to recognize that we owe our existence to the kindness of others. Our staff is generous with their skills. Our donors are generous with their gifts. Our volunteers give over and above in time and love. And our citizens generously share their lives with us and with each other every day. But when I think of generosity, two stories quickly come to mind—and one of them involves my dad. I've said that he was a doctor, and he was a very good one. Many years ago, late one evening, he received a phone call from a man who was not a patient of his, but whose wife had fallen ill. The couple was not able to drive and the caller felt his wife needed immediate medical assistance. The man was angry—he read my Dad the riot act and said "You blankety-blank doctors think you are too good to make house calls anymore. I've called three doctors and no one will help her. She may be dying and you don't even care!" When Dad got him calmed down, he asked where he lived, retrieved his medical bag from storage, and went to see them.

You might be wondering what this has to do with Brookwood. Many years later I received a call from an attorney who told me that the gentlemen who called my father that night had died, and that in his will, left something for "that place that Dr. Tuttle's daughter

"A surprise gift—so meaningful—so needed."

started." I had never heard of the man, but he was a small business owner with no children. I told the attorney that we were very, very grateful because this was in our early days when "outsiders" didn't think that this program would work and we were really struggling financially. As one of our board members said "we are constantly trying to "squeeze the buffalo off of each nickel." The attorney said, "You are really going to appreciate this gift then. My client left you this gift in his will because fifty years ago, your Dad gave him a gift. Your Dad made a house call when Doctors had quit making house calls and that was greatly appreciated." I thanked him again, and he said, "Aren't you going to ask how much he left for you?"

I hadn't asked him because I thought it might be impolite. I imagined it might be a few hundred dollars, and I knew we could use each dollar he left. I then said of course I would like to know if you don't mind. He said: "$108,000." I was shocked, joyous, and ever so grateful, both for my father's generous response to this man in his *time of need, and for this man's great generosity in return. That gift was a lifesaver.* A surprise gift—so meaningful—so needed.

It's not the size of a gift that makes it generous, though. It's the heart behind it. I've been asked before, "What's the biggest monetary gift you've ever received at Brookwood?"—a question I find almost impossible to answer. But if pressed, I might tell you about this one: One of the first gifts that ever came our way was from a family with a son at Briarwood. He had cerebral palsy, and was one of the sweetest young men I have ever met. His parents were wonderful, too. One day they made an appointment to see me, and after talking for a while about the great progress their son was making in school, they said, "We are so excited about your plan for 'the country place' that we want to give a gift to help get it started. This startled me because I knew their son was on scholarship and their financial situation was difficult. "We've talked about this for a long time," the father said, "and we want to give you $10 a month for a year." I could barely recover from hearing in depth, what they were saying. Generosity comes, you see, in all shapes and sizes—and love shared with others quite often returns to you in surprising ways.

Love shared with others quite often returns to you in surprising ways.

TRUST

Trust plays a major part in establishing relationships and relationships are strengthened through trust. Trust begins with trusting God, and the staff trusting each other and through these actions our citizens learn to trust us. These actions are critically important in all we do and teach at Brookwood. It is one of the most important things that *we must develop*, stimulate *and cultivate*. Trust goes from God to us, and us to God, and then from us to our fellow man. So many of our special needs adults and children have had really very few successful ventures which means that they are often fearful of trying anything new. Most of them have experienced failure: failure to measure up to Mom or Dad's expectations, failure to be accepted by others, failure to excel at anything, and worse than that, failure to measure up to their *own* expectations and dreams. Before we can teach a citizen anything, we have to *earn* his or her trust. This focus on being trustworthy has brought so many blessings to our community. Trust can sometimes be learned through the auditory input but *that is not as effective a way to learn it as having it felt by action, words and deeds.*

Trust, too, comes in many ways. Because they trusted us, River Oaks Garden Club and the Garden Club of Houston gave us our first four greenhouses that were the catalyst to our horticulture enterprise. St. Luke's United Methodist Church trusted us to be good stewards and gave the "temporary" building we are still using thirty years later. Many generous donors have trusted that our community really helps our citizens; and our

> **Every day our citizens teach without speaking, minister without preaching, and lift each other up, though their own bodies are weak.**

citizens trust their teachers to put them in situations where they will learn and grow with success. Our citizens contribute to an atmosphere of trust by doing what they say they are going to do because they have seen and felt others do what they said they were going to do. Agape is practiced by being kind, thoughtful, and supportive of one another even when no one but God is watching. All of the above contributes to building and maintaining *Relationships of Trust*. Our community would not survive without trust—but with it, we all thrive.

So these are some of the values we try to live by—trust, generosity, interdependence, compassion, perspective, celebration, patience, life-long learning, a positive focus, and unconditional love. It's an amazing list, and we are surrounded by examples of each of these important concepts. Every day our citizens teach without speaking, minister without preaching, and lift each other up, though their own bodies are weak. That's the Brookwood way. That's God's way.

A FAMILY AFFAIR

B rookwood became not only a home for Vicki, but also an invitation for our daughters Vita and Vivian to venture into the social service field, and for Dave to become Brookwood's longest-serving *pro bono* attorney.

The three sisters:
(Left to right) Vivian, Vicki, and Vita.

Vicki was the seed, the reason this community we call Brookwood began. Dave provided that caring, steady hand, participating unwaveringly in Vicki's care all the while providing the finances to put "food on the table and Pappagalos in the closet" for his family of five. He provided the support that our family needed from the moment this journey began.

When I look back on the early years of Brookwood, I don't know what we would have done without Vita and many of our pioneer employees like Rosemary's sons, Hayden and Steve Larson. Instead of doing a little bit of everything they did a *lot* of everything. Steve helped start the horticulture division of Brookwood, and Vita set up the business office and the procedures that we had to follow to become efficient and compliant with our financial operations. Hayden was the first sculptor for our stone-casting division, and he and Steve were both resourceful workers. Vita later took over the horticulture division after Steve left; she worked long hours for practically no pay, and she did it with joy. Rosemary's daughter Dea was not a staff member, but she, too, has been an important part of Brookwood: Dea became a lawyer and financial advisor and now serves on our Board of Directors.

Vita graduated from SMU and could do just about anything. She was key in overseeing our programs and monitoring their progress; she hired, supervised and trained new staff. In spite of the typical little bumps in the road, she was determined to provide a successful *home* for her sister and the many other citizens she had come to love. She ultimately applied what she learned from her experiences at Brookwood in a position as the Executive Director of the Ft. Bend County Women's Center where she serves today. Her work strengthens our community, and demonstrates the love for others that she both witnessed and exhibited from the time she was a little girl.

Vivian also has found her life's calling in helping others. She attended "that school in Austin" (the University of Texas) and received her degree in special education. A woman of many interests and talents, she also started and worked in her own private business—a very successful children's clothing enterprise. Her background in special education, her skills in business, along with her experience as the mother of a special needs child made her an obvious choice when we were contemplating who would help lead Brookwood into the future. It didn't take the pro bono headhunter doing our search very long to begin looking in her direction! Vivian is now executive director of The Brookwood Community. Her passion and dedication to the quality and success of our programs is evident every day. Her diligent emphases on succession planning, solidifying the culture, and communicating our mission are essential to making the future of Brookwood secure.

My husband and each of our three daughters had significant contributions to make to the Brookwood story, each with their own seed to sow for Brookwood's beginning and its ongoing growth. It is clear to me now that

God knew from the start exactly where this journey would lead us. The hidden treasures that have unfolded along the way are certainly *beyond all human understanding!*

God knew from the start exactly where this journey would lead us.

So Brookwood began as a family affair, and that small family became an extended family that has continued to grow. Today, including citizens and staff, the Brookwood family is several hundred strong—and each of us has more seeds to sow. And, from the beginning, as we have engaged with the community, others have been deeply generous in sharing their gifts to help us as well. Because of this generosity, the Brookwood family is growing!

BUSINESSES LEND A HAND

In 2014, the owner of a major furniture company partnered with us by providing a 12,500 square foot area for a Brookwood gift shop, an on-site greenhouse, and a classroom/art studio for adults with special needs in his newest store in Fort Bend County, TX. This company's generosity has made it possible for Brookwood to employ more citizens, contribute significantly to The Brookwood Community's operating budget, and help more adults with special needs gain meaningful life and job skills.

Collaboration with another local institution began with an introduction by Fran, a dear friend and a member on our Advancement Board. Fran knew that we had a great interest in the good work of this group, and invited their entire Executive Committee out to Brookwood. Because education is their primary focus, she wanted them to see that the educational processes we were employing for our citizens could and should be applied to an ever-expanding group of folks with special needs. As a result, these good folks have taken us under their wing, affirming the educational opportunities that we offer. We are thrilled to work with these two fine groups (in addition to many, many others) in championing education, scholarships and opportunity.

Another local partnership Brookwood enjoys is our relationship with a historic Houston hat company. After operating in downtown Houston for 100 years, this company's store was relocated to our Brookshire store with sales to benefit the citizens of Brookwood. This fine hatter helps to sustain the needs of our community, just as sales from our horticulture and craft enterprises do. We welcome local partnerships such as these and hope to cultivate more of them in the future.

A little further from home, a Brookwood presence in Georgetown, Texas, has taken root. In August of 2011, Light Texas, an entrepreneurial vocational initiative in Georgetown came under the umbrella of Brookwood and became BiG (Brookwood in Georgetown), serving adults with special needs in the Central Texas area. Recently Brookwood in Georgetown began to operate as an independent 501(c) (3) organization, and we are proud to have been a part of their growth toward independence.

As God nudges Brookwood out into the world, we are excited to see what his plans are. While we know there will be inevitable puddles on the path, our journey so far has taught us to trust so much more than I ever would have imagined possible. The Vickis of the world have a place where they can be appreciated and loved and do meaningful work, just as they are. The message is spreading, the seeds we have all planted at Brookwood are growing, and the blossoms on the tree are heavenly gifts that truly reflect God's love for all of us.

A CLOSING CHALLENGE

I have been told by those who know that an author never finishes a book and an artist never finishes a painting. I think I now know what they mean. As I go over the stories I have shared with you and think about the myriad kindnesses and generous gifts of prayer, time, energy, service, and money they represent, I think of this book as just the tip of the iceberg. I worry a great deal that with fifty years of wonderful examples, I have inadvertently left out important happenings or people who have been so instrumental in the development of Brookwood.

But however incomplete my tale, I hope that after reading this story about The Brookwood Community you may have added another dimension to your perspective about people with special needs. I hope that you, like us, have been convinced that the folks that were deemed "unteachable" are indeed teachable—*if* we are creative enough, determined enough, and persistent enough to take on that challenge that offers such great rewards.

> **The horizons of what can be are greater than we ever imagined.**

We at Brookwood have come to realize that the horizons of what *can be* are greater than we ever imagined. At times we may miss some of His gifts because we are too busy to notice, because we were too worried about what *might* happen, or because we judged them with the world's unknowing eye. Thankfully our awareness of God's presence throughout this journey has awakened us to His gifts, and when we feel that familiar nudge, we are constantly on the lookout for his message. We have learned to pay attention to nudges.

Before I close, I'd like to bring you up to date on our daughter Vicki, the blessing who became the catalyst for Briarwood and for Brookwood. Vicki is now fifty-nine. She has had a difficult life medically speaking and is still what you might call medically fragile. We continue fighting her debilitating seizures and their side effects, but in spite of these, she is enjoying a good life.

From my office, I have the privilege to watch our citizens move from work studios to lunch or physical fitness, and I am able to see agape love at work: some citizens pushing wheel chairs, some with a friend by their side for support, and Vicki walking vigorously and with enthusiasm to work. She has purpose, security, and love. She is active and very purposeful about her job. She is not weighed down with problems or unresolved issues. She is not jealous, or greedy, or prideful; and, in her world, she feels like a queen. God is her Burden Bearer and will be with her through this life and on into eternity!

Once we were able to put Him in the driver's seat we stopped trying to "fix" Vicki because she is not broken—she just walks to the beat of a different drummer. The rest of our family has enjoyed some of these same treasures, although not as thoroughly as Vicki, because we still feel the urge to be in control and we battle the demons of anxiety, worry, and fear. All that aside, with Vicki's wordless leadership, we have been afforded opportunities and insight that we would never have otherwise known.

I hope those of you who are family, friends, educators, medical professionals, leaders of similar organizations, or individuals who care about a person with special needs will take advantage of our mistakes and our successes and become a part of the ever-widening circle working together to make this world a better place.

Everybody's got a seed to sow. I pray that the future of Brookwood will hold still more life-giving seeds like the ones so many people have shared with us already. And wherever you are, whatever the situation in your life may be, in your family or in your work, I hope that you remember that you have an important seed also...

Don't just keep that seed—Plant it—Nourish it—Let it grow.

God will do the rest!

Aerial view of Brookwood.

THE PROCEEDS FROM THE SALE

OF EACH COPY OF THIS BOOK

GO TO BROOKWOOD, ITS CITIZENS,

AND ITS OUTREACH PROGRAMS.

APPENDIX

THE BROOKWOOD COMMUNITY

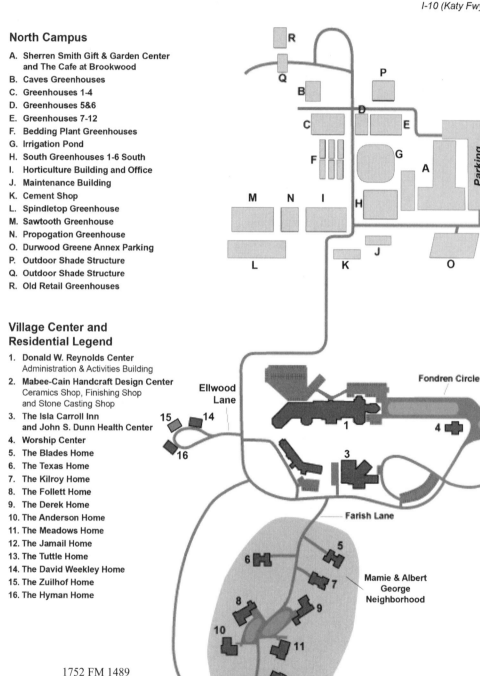

I-10 (Katy Fwy)

North Campus

A. Sherren Smith Gift & Garden Center and The Cafe at Brookwood
B. Caves Greenhouses
C. Greenhouses 1-4
D. Greenhouses 5&6
E. Greenhouses 7-12
F. Bedding Plant Greenhouses
G. Irrigation Pond
H. South Greenhouses 1-6 South
I. Horticulture Building and Office
J. Maintenance Building
K. Cement Shop
L. Spindletop Greenhouse
M. Sawtooth Greenhouse
N. Propogation Greenhouse
O. Durwood Greene Annex Parking
P. Outdoor Shade Structure
Q. Outdoor Shade Structure
R. Old Retail Greenhouses

Village Center and Residential Legend

1. Donald W. Reynolds Center
   Administration & Activities Building
2. Mabee-Cain Handcraft Design Center
   Ceramics Shop, Finishing Shop
   and Stone Casting Shop
3. The Isla Carroll Inn
   and John S. Dunn Health Center
4. Worship Center
5. The Blades Home
6. The Texas Home
7. The Kilroy Home
8. The Follett Home
9. The Derek Home
10. The Anderson Home
11. The Meadows Home
12. The Jamail Home
13. The Tuttle Home
14. The David Weekley Home
15. The Zuilhof Home
16. The Hyman Home

1752 FM 1489
Brookshire, Texas 77423
281-375-2100
www.brookwoodcommunity.org

RESOURCES

Barron Neurological Foundation. February 23, 2016. http://www.supportbarrow.org.

Bethel Institution. February 23, 2016. http://en.wikipedia.org/wiki/Bethel_Institution.

Bethel Institution. February 23, 2016. http://www.bethel.eu.

Briarwood School. February 23, 2016. http://www.briarwoodschool.org.

Brookwood Community. February 23, 2016. http://www.brookwoodcommunity.org.

Celey Colorado Camp. February 23, 2016. http://www.celey.com.

Dravecky, Dave. February 23, 2016. http://www.davedravecky.com.

Gold, Marc. *Try Another Way Training Manual.* Research Publishing, 1980. http://www.discovery-ability.com/try-another-way-marc-gold.

"Marc Gold and Try Another Way." February 23, 2016. You Tube video. http://www.youtube.com/watch?v-prUIcZ8pXNA.

Harrelson, Woody. North Channel Star. February 23, 2016. http://www.northchannel-star.com/2014/03.

Hillman, James. Wikipedia. February 23, 2016. https://en.wikipedia.org/wiki/James_Hillman.

Houston Livestock Show and Rodeo. February 23, 2016. http://www.rodeohouston.com.

The Georgiana Rodiger Center, Inc. February 23, 2016. http://www.rodigercenter.org/home6.

Kephart, Newell C. Biblio. February 23, 2016. http:// www.biblio.com.

The Slow Learner in the Classroom. Columbus, Ohio: Charles E. Merrill Publishers, rpt. 1968.

University of Missouri – St. Louis. February 23, 2016. http:// www.umsl.edu/.

University of Northern Colorado. February 23, 2016. http://www.unco.edu/library.

Lamb's Farm. Libertyville, Illinois. http://www.lambsfarms.org.

Lovaas, Ivor. Lovaas Institute. February 23, 2016. http://www.lovaas.com/.

McIngvale, Jim. Wikipedia. February 23, 2016. https://wikipedia.org/wiki/Jim_McIngvale.

Mesibov, Gary B. Wikipedia. February 23, 2016. https://en.wikipedia/wiki/Gary_B._Mesibov.

The University of North Carolina. TEACCH Autism Program. February 23, 2016. http://www.teacch.com.

Nutcracker Market. February 23, 2016. http://www.houstonballet.org/Nutcracker-Market/Nutcracker-Market-Overview/.

Radler, D. H. *Success Through Play: How to Prepare Your Child for School Achievement and Enjoy It.* New York: Harper & Row, 1960.

Shudde Bros Hatters. February 23, 2016. http://www.shudde.com.

Smith, Michael W. February 23, 2016. www.michaelwsmith.com.

"Everybody's Got a Seed to Sow."

"Michael W. Smith & The African Children's Choir." You Tube video.

February 23, 2016. http://www.youtube.com/watch?v-irUzutYx5r0.

BROOKWOOD

Our declaration of dependence

For all we are, all we have and all we do, we are graciously and confidently dependent on God, and on the men and women God calls by name to take part in the mission of Brookwood.

Our respect for each individual

We see every individual as a unique creation of a wise and loving God, deserving not only of our abiding patience and respect, but of boundless awe. We cherish diversity in all forms and eschew narrow-minded notions of normalcy.

Our devotion to learning

We grant persons in our community the freedom to learn in the ways best suited to them. In turn, we ask each person to give his best at all times. We expect to discover gifts in everyone.

Our promise to share

We pledge that what we learn we will share, within our community and with others called to serve God's most remarkable people. By what we learn and share, millions will benefit.

Our regard for industry

We believe that God calls us all to meaningful work to contribute to our world. We engage in our business enterprises with zeal and a commitment to do things safely or not at all, and manage our affairs prudently, to ensure the Brookwood brand is strong today and for years to come.

Our pledge to employees

We strive to attract, nurture and retain the finest employees at work in our field. We give them authority to use their capabilities to the fullest extent in serving this community and advancing the mission. We treat one another with dignity. And we listen to each other with an open mind regardless of title or tenure.

Our appreciation for support

We regard that the people and business that support our operations, buy our products and serve on our leadership and staff as sent to us by God. We are inspired by their service, instructed through their wisdom, and humbled by their benevolence. We resist government monies to protect our autonomy and heighten our efficiency.

Our aspirations for excellence

While our endeavors present us uncommon challenges, we nonetheless strive for excellence in everything we undertake. Our lives are testimonies to our Maker, so we demand the best of ourselves. We aim to be the premier residential, entrepreneurial and educational community for adults with disabilities.

Our practice of reciprocity

We feel privileged to give and to receive as a community, and believe that both acts have transforming power for us and the world. By being grateful recipients, we acknowledge our humble reliance on God and on others. By our disciplined learning and excellent work, we give back and enrich other lives as well as our own.

Our assurance to families

We pledge to the families of our citizens that we will cherish their loved ones as our own—instructing, inspiring and helping them realize their God-given talents as uniquely created children of God. We will ask God to show us the work to do, and give us His strength and wisdom to uphold these commandments.

MILESTONES

1956
Vicki Streit born to Yvonne and David Streit

1957
Vicki became ill with encephalitis and meningitis due to complications
from the mumps resulting in severe brain damage

1957—1964
Vicki hospitalized numerous times with severe seizures
leaving her near death

1964—1966
Yvonne Streit traveled to numerous universities and programs
that were working with children with special needs. Met Dr. Kephart
at Purdue University who introduced a transforming
educational perspective for this population

1966
Yvonne began working with six children with functional disabilities
in her backyard based on an accumulation of the various programs
she had learned in her travels throughout the United States.

1967
Moved program from her backyard to Memorial Drive
Baptist Church, Houston, Texas

1968
Moved to Le Petite Nursery School

1969

Moved to local church school

1970

Moved to St. Philip Presbyterian Church

1973

School building opened with the official name of The Briarwood School

---

1978

The Brookwood Community envisioned by founders.
Search for land location began

1981

Acquired 475 acre site in Brookshire, Texas on December 31, 1981,
for The Brookwood Community

1982

New construction on nursery area began, including four greenhouses,
pump house and reservoir for irrigation.

1983

Workshop and office at Horticulture Center completed—
day program began.

1984

One-acre tree farm and growing area for 1500 containerized trees
completed, farm house occupied as Administrative
Center and Enterprise production areas.

1985

The Inn and first residential homes completed.
These homes provided housing for home teachers and 28 students.
Two more greenhouses completed.

1986

Two additional bedding plant greenhouses completed.

1988

Multi-purpose building which accommodates Hand-Crafts
Enterprise and Brookwood's business office,
and two additional residential homes completed.

1989

Construction of four more bedding plant greenhouses and
six hydroponic tomato greenhouses completed,
bringing total greenhouse square footage to 56,800.

1991

Two additional residential homes completed and dedicated.

1994

A $4.8 million Challenge grant was met providing funds to build the
Mabee-Cain building, a Garden Statuary Workshop, a maintenance
building, and the Sherren Smith Gift and Garden Center.

1995

10th Anniversary of the first residential citizens joining the community.
Two additional residential homes completed,
bringing a total number to seven.

1996

Expanded Mabee-Cain crafts building

1997

A $5.5 million grant from The Donald W. Reynolds Foundation funds
construction of The Reynolds Building, which houses a Visitors' Center,
a cafetorium, a gymnasium and water therapy areas, general activities
and classroom space as well as administrative offices.

1998
Construction begins on Worship Center and two new greenhouses.

1999
Worship Center completed and dedicated. Climate-controlled horticulture
center completed. Café at the Inn opens to the public.

2000
The log-cabin Sherren Smith Gift and Garden Center
burned to the ground. Houston supporters launched fundraising
to rebuild the SSGGC, the addition of a state-of-the-art propagation
greenhouse and a new 27,000 sq. ft. greenhouse.

2001
The new Sherren Smith Gift and Garden Center and Café dedicated.

2004
Renovation of Inn is completed.

2005
20th Anniversary of the first citizens joining the community;
The Inn rededicated as the Isla Carroll Inn and the John S. Dunn
Health Center. Barbara Bush speaks at the dedication.
Campaign to grow Brookwood's endowment began.

2007
The Weekly Home is completed and dedicated.

2008
The Hyman Home is dedicated as part of Retirement with a
Purpose Project, and renovation on residential homes completed.

2009
Fund-raising campaign to underwrite expansion of Gift and
Garden Center and Café is completed.

2010

Commemoration of 25th Anniversary of The Brookwood Community.
Construction to expand the Gift and Garden Center, Café,
and Welcome Center is completed.

2012

Ten-acre property adjacent to Brookwood site with frontage
on FM 1489 acquired for future expansion.

2013

Brookwood launches the "The Brookwood Way"
network days conferences to exchange ideas, share information
and encourage peer organizations throughout the U.S.
and the world in the field of disabilities.

2014

Plans formulated for new retail venues with day citizen work
programs in Ft. Bend and Montgomery Counties

2015

Celebration of Brookwood's 30th anniversary and
the opening of the retail gift and garden center and artisan/work
program in Ft. Bend County.

2016

Brookwood looks forward to the future!

ACKNOWLEDGMENTS

I'm sure that many people feel as I do, that it is very difficult to choose the right words in order to transmit the overwhelming sense of gratitude you feel when you want someone to know how deeply moved you are by a kindness, a gift, or their support in a singular or a multitude of ways. It is not easy to find those right words that will truly make these folks understand what others want them to know. I guess that is why we use the two words "Thank You" so often. So to the many people who have helped put this book together and to the many others who may have inadvertently been left out, I say THANK YOU:

- For God's Grace in His guidance and willingness to put up with our jillions of mistakes and to help us learn from them.
- Once again to my family: Dave, Vita, Vivian, to my parents Vita & Dewey Tuttle, Jean Farge, and, of course, to Vicki.
- To Brookwood Staff, parents, citizens, volunteers, donors, advisors, and mentors past and present, whose contributions have helped put this complex puzzle together. Their individual and collective puzzle pieces have been the building blocks of Brookwood.
- To Barbara Bush for her encouragement and for opening doors to advisors and consultants.
- To Debbie Bragg, a fantastic transcriber and reader.

- ❖ To Rossitsa Israel and Chris Martin of 1.618 Multimedia for their many, many contributions.
- ❖ To Susan Buddeke and Rahul Mehta for the use of their homes as retreats to work on the book in "peace and quiet."
- ❖ To Michael Hart for his many hours of waiting to catch the right time for his gift of photo journalism for this book.
- ❖ To Tita Caveness for letting us use each and every newsletter that she has saved since Brookwood began.
- ❖ To Heather Hartt and Keystone Consulting Group for their constant assistance in keeping us and our computers on the same track.
- ❖ To Grace Moceri, Jessica Powers, Yara Suki, and Amy Vandaveer for their expertise and guidance.
- ❖ To Steve Barnhill for his thoughtful and insightful commentary on the heart of Brookwood illustrated in the Cornerstone Document.
- ❖ To Leigh McLeroy for her expertise in editing and for going above and beyond the call of duty.
- ❖ To the people, the stories, and the angels that may have inadvertently been left out.
- ❖ And with a huge hug and lots of thanks to Lucy Chambers and the staff of Bright Sky Press for their guidance, patience, and perseverance with this project.

Located in Brookshire, Texas, 40 miles
west of downtown Houston,
The Brookwood Community is
a non-profit (501(c) (3) residential facility
and vocational program.

For additional information on
the Brookwood Community,
please visit Brookwood's website at:
www.brookwoodcommunity.org